Yu-dofu (Simmered Tofu) ··············32
Natto & Fried Leaf Mustard ··········32
Shrimp & Egg Custard ···············33
• **Reproduce "Tofu Hyakuchin"** ········33–35
Thunder Tofu/Clear Tofu/Puffy Tofu
《**Western Style**》
Tofu Stuffed Cabbage Rolls ···········36
Okara Soup ·····················37
Toasted Koori-dofu ················37
Tofu & Pine Nut Salad ··············38
Natto Pizza ·····················38
• **Let's Make Momen-dofu**·········40–41
《**Chinese Style**》
Chili Sauce of Tofu & Shrimp ·········42
Natto Shaomai ···················43
Stir-fried Toasted Tofu ··············43
Noodles Topped with Natto & Nira ·····44
Green Soup of Tofu················44
Fried Rice with Tofu ···············45
Chinese-style Salad with Koori-dofu ·····45
《**Cakes & Cookies**》
Okara & Prune Cookie ·············46
Sponge Cake of Koori-dofu ···········47
Tofu & Powdered Green Tea Dumpling ···47
• **Tofu Dishes from Okinawa** ·······48–49
Goya Champuru/Ukararichi/Ujira-tofu

Carrot Potage ···················59
Chinese-style Soy Milk Soup··········59
《**Yuba**》
Yuba with Vinegared Sesame ·········60
Yuba with Cod Roe & Milk ··········60
Deep-fried Yuba & Chicken Breasts········60
《**Daizu Moyashi**》
Moyashi Salad ···················62
Moyashi & Mentaiko ···············63
Curry & Moyashi ·················63
《**Kinako**》
Potato Rice Cake coated with Kinako··········64
Twisted Kinako ··················64

Chapter 3
OTHER FOODS PROCESSED FROM SOYBEANS

《**Atsu-age**》
Gadogado Salad ··················50
Cheese Piccata ···················51
Fried Atsu-age with Sweet Vinegar ······52
Atsu-age, Greens & Young Sardines ·····52
《**Abura-age**》
Abura-age & Julienne Vegetables ·······54
Zenmai Rolled in Abura-age ··········55
Grilled Abura-age ················55
《**Miso**》
Chilled Cucumber Soup ·············56
Braised Chicken & Daikon ···········57
Dried Daikon with Miso Mayonnaise ······57
《**Soy Milk**》
Littleneck Clam Chowder ···········58

■BASIC PREPARATION ···········4–5
Parboiling Soybeans / Draining Tofu / Reconstituting Koori-dofu / Removing Oil from Abura-age / Toasting Okara

■ARTICLES
• **Effects of Soybeans (1)** ···········21
Clean the Inside of Blood Vessels and Beat Adult Diseases
• **Effects of Soybeans (2)** ···········29
Soybeans make Bones Strong and Prevent Colon Cancer
• **Effects of Soybeans (3)** ···········39
Soybeans are Good for Beauty and Figure
• **Effects of Soybeans (4)** ···········53
Develop Tireless Strength
• **Chinese Cheese 'Furu'** ···········53

LET'S EAT MORE SOYBEANS FOR LONGEVITY

Soybeans are popularly called 'mame' in Japanese, and the expression 'live like mame' is used to mean 'to be in good health.' In former days, we used to send a box of soybeans in return for a present received on celebratory occasions with wishes for good health. At New Year's, black soybeans are customarily eaten to pray for a healthy year. On the day of *setsubun* (the day before the beginning of spring), people drive away devils by throwing roasted soybeans and eat as many beans as their age to ensure their health. In this way, soybeans have been closely related to Japanese daily life.

In terms of nutrients, soybeans are a valuable source of protein. They are processed in various ways; *miso* (soybeans paste), *shoyu* (soy sauce), *natto* (fermented soybeans), *tofu* (soybean curd), *yuba*(sheets of dried soybean casein), *kinako* (soybean flour) and so on. Japanese people are completely dependent on soybeans, which are basis of their dietary habits.

Remarkable Nutrients and New Effects

In order to enjoy a long life, we have to prevent such degenerative diseases as arteriosclerosis, hypertension and myocardial infarction. In this respect, the nutritional value and properties of soybeans have recently come to be the focus of the people's attention. So far soybeans have been called 'the meat in the field' and valued as highprotein food. In addition to this, their new effects have recently been discovered. They contain lecithin and saponin which help reduce blood cholesterol. The westernized eating habits of Japan have raised new questions about the increase in the blood cholesterol, but the dietary fiber and ingredients of soybeans were found to go a long way toward lowering it.

One of the topics talked about recently is osteoporosis, which is caused through lack of calcium. Such patients are liable to have their thighbones broken and this disease is said to account for about 20 percent of bedridden elderly people. Milk and dried young sardines have been known as popular sources of calcium, but one of the ingredients of soybeans, isofurabonoido, has recently been discovered to prevent the outflow of calcium from bones. It also strikes a balance of female sex hormones, so it is good news for those suffering from menopausal disorders.

The vitamin K_2 contained in *natto* plays an important role in making healthy bones. Those people living in the eastern part of Japan are said to experience fewer cases of bone fractures than people in the western part, and this fact seems to owe to the habits of eating *natto*.

As perfect food of longevity, soybeans are drawing attention of the world's scholars. That is because they are interested in the Japanese way of living, especially the eating habits of people enjoying longevity. In the United States, *tofu* is sold at supermarkets, under the motto, 'let's eat white meat (tofu) in place of red meat (steak).' It is also served at school meals.

Enjoy Wide Varieties of Cooking

In Japan, the most popular soybean dishes have been boiled beans cooked with vegetables and other ingredients. Soybeans are good for health, but if served only boiled beans, those accustomed to westernized food will be tired of the menu. If simple new menus are worked out, they will go well with rice and bread and more soybean dishes will come to be served at the table. This book introduces plenty of menus, Japanese, Western and Chinese styles. The author will be more than delighted if this book inspires your interest in soybeans. Eat soybeans for long life.

About the author:

A Doctor of Science, nutritionist and lecturer at Women's Junior College of Nippon College of Physical Education. The diet adviser to the professional baseball team, the Yomiuri Giants. She plays an active part on TV and a regular contributor to magazines.

Key Nutrients of Soybeans and Processed Foods

(per 100 g)   Data from "Standard Tables of Food Composition, 1996"

	Calories (kcal)	Protein (g)	Fat (g)	Glucose (g)	Calcium (mg)	Iron (mg)	Sodium (mg)	Potassium (mg)	Vitamin A (IU)	Vitamin E (mg)	Vitamin B₁ (mg)	Vitamin B₂ (mg)	Vitamin C (mg)
Soybeans (boiled)	180	16.0	9.0	7.6	70	2.0	1	570	Ø		0.22	0.09	Ø
Edamame (young soybeans, boiled)	139	11.4	6.6	7.4	70	1.7	1	570	55		0.27	0.14	27
Kinugoshi-dofu (silken tofu)	58	5.0	3.3	1.7	90	1.1	4	140	0	0.2	0.10	0.04	0
Momen-dofu (firm tofu)	77	6.8	5.0	0.8	120	1.4	3	85	0	0.4	0.07	0.03	0
Koori-dofu (freeze-dried tofu)	533	50.2	33.4	5.3	590	9.4	8	32	Ø	3.0	0.02	0.03	0
Natto (fermented soybeans)	200	16.5	10.0	9.8	90	3.3	2	660	0	0.9	0.07	0.56	0
Okara (tofu lees)	89	4.8	3.6	6.4	100	1.2	4	230	Ø	0.4	0.11	0.04	0
Atsu-age (thick deep-fried tofu)	151	10.7	11.3	1.0	240	2.6	3	120	0	1.1	0.07	0.03	0
Abura-age (thin deep-fried tofu)	388	18.6	33.1	2.8	300	4.2	10	55	0	2.1	0.06	0.03	0
Light Miso (salty)	192	12.5	6.0	19.4	100	4.0	4900	380	0	1.0	0.03	0.10	0
Tounyu (soymilk)	46	3.6	2.0	2.9	15	1.2	2	90	0	0.2	0.03	0.02	0
Yuba (tofu casein, raw)	231	21.8	13.7	4.1	90	3.6	4	290	Ø		0.17	0.09	0
Yuba (dried)	511	53.2	28.0	8.9	200	8.1	13	850	20		0.20	0.08	0
Moyashi (soybean sprouts)	54	5.4	2.2	2.6	33	0.7	4	240	Ø	0.9	0.13	0.10	8
Kinako (soybean flour)	437	35.5	23.4	26.4	250	9.2	1	1900	Ø	1.7	0.76	0.26	0

Note: Ø means almost nil.

BASIC PREPARATION

● Draining Tofu

● Parboiling Soybeans

Get fresh beans and parboil them beforehand. Drain and keep in the refrigerator for later use. The amount of beans will be doubled when parboiled. Green and black soybeans should also be parboiled.

Draining is an important procedure to improve the flavor and retain an attractive shape. If you skip this step, the tofu will become watery and fall apart while boiling. On the other hand, if you drain to excess, the tofu will become unpleasant to the taste and lose flavor.

① Wash 1 cup soybeans, soak in 3 cups water and let stand overnight.

② Cook the whole over strong heat. When it comes to a boil, lower the heat and simmer for about 1 hour.

③ When the liquid is reduced, add water. When the beans become soft enough to be crushed with fingers, transfer to a bamboo colander.

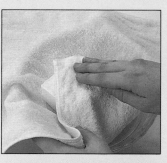

⟨In the refrigerator⟩
Wrap the tofu in a thick towel. Place it on a platter and keep in the refrigerator for about 2 hours.

⟨With a microwave oven⟩
① Place the tofu on a heatroof platter and heat without wrap. (Heat 3 minutes per block)

② Spread paper towel on a bamboo colander. Place the tofu on top and let stand for about 10 minutes.

Careful preparation is important for an attractive appearance and savory taste. Try to understand the characteristics of soybeans and tofu and make much use of them.

Reconstituting Koori-dofu (Freeze-dried Tofu)

It is important to reconstitute the koori-dofu (freeze-dried tofu) completely. If incomplete, it tends to be unplesant to the taste, and not well seasoned. Koori-dofu, which is easy to reconstitute, has come to be available recently, so try it.

① Place koori-dofu in a bowl and cover with lukewarm water.

② Let it stand for some time, and then wash, pressing with hands, and squeeze out the water.

③ When reconstituted completely, it swells and lose its color (right in the photo).

Removing Oil from Abura-age (Thin deep-fried Tofu)

Remove excess oil from the abura-age. It makes the tofu light and easy to season.

Place the abura-age on a bamboo colander, pour boiled water over and drain.

Toasting Okara (Tofu Lees)

When making a baked cake or dressing, toast the tofu lees beforehand to avoid a watery finish. Okara is easily spoiled, so preserve by freezing after toasting.

Place the okara in a heat-proof dish, cover with plastic wrap and heat for 3 minutes per $3\frac{1}{2}$ oz (100 g). Remove the wrap. Break the okara up into pieces with chopsticks. Reheat without wrap for 1 minute and 30 seconds. Repeat breaking up until completely loosened.

Chapter 1

SOYBEAN COOKING

Called 'the meat in the field,' soybeans are a good source of high protein and a well-balanced food. They are cooked as they are or mashed and steamed or used in a variety of interesting dishes. Presented here are recipes arranged according to Japanese, Western and Chinese styles.

Steamed Rolls with Edamame

Ingredients (4 servings)

1 cup edamame (young soybeans) boiled
3½ oz (100 g) ground chicken
4 eggs
½ carrot
1¾ oz (50 g) string beans
½ onion
⅔ cup breadcrumbs
pinch sugar
1 Tbsp butter
cornstarch, salt, oil, lettuce

[Calories 280 kcal., Protein 18.4 g] for one person, et seq.

Method: 1. Boil the edamame (young soybeans) according to page 13. Take out of the pods.
2. Add a pinch of salt and sugar to 3 eggs and mix. Heat oil in a frying pan and cook soft scrambled eggs (photo 1).
3. Mince the onion and stir-fry with butter. Cut the carrot into long sticks and boil with string beans in salted water.
4. Put the edamame in a food processor and mix for 5~6 seconds. In a bowl combine the edamame, ground meat, onion, 1 egg, breadcrumbs, a pinch of salt (photo 2) and mix all well.
5. Spread aluminum foil on a makisu (bamboo mat) and coat with oil. Spread **4** on the foil. Sprinkle with cornstarch and add **2** (photo 3). Sprinkle with cornstarch again. Place the carrot and string beans in the center and roll (photo 4). Wrap in foil and make holes at an interval of 1⅕″ (3 cm) with a bamboo skewer.
6. Steam in a steamer over medium heat for about 30 minutes. Cut into pieces and serve with lettuce.

Daizu (soybeans):
The color of high-quality soybeans are yellow or yellowish white and they have glossy texture. New beans are put on the market in October or November.

Aodaizu (green soybeans):
A kind of soybeans. It is also called 'hitashi-mame.' They have a black point in the center and are flat in shape.

Edamame (young soybeans in pods):
Young beans harvested while the pods are green. The best season is summer, but frozen beans are available all year round.

Kuromame (black beans):
A kind of soybeans. The skin is black and they have a black point in the center.

Soybeans & Hijiki Seaweed

Ingredients (4 servings)

2 cups boiled soybeans	1 small carrot
⅜ oz (10 g) hijiki sea-weed	some dashi stock
	5 Tbsp shoyu
3 dried shiitake mush-rooms	3 Tbsp sugar
	2 Tbsp sake (rice wine)
1 abura-age (deep-fried tofu)	1½ Tbsp sesame oil

[Calories 290 kcal., Protein 17.0 g]

Method: 1. Rinse the hijiki and soak in 1 cup of water for 20 minutes. Drain. Cover the shiitake with water until soft. Cut off the stems and slice the caps. Reserve the soaking water.
2. Remove the excess oil from the abura-age according to page 5. Cut the abura-age and carrot into julienne strips.
3. Heat the sesame oil in a pan and sauté the hijiki, shiitake, abura-age and carrot (photo 1).
4. When the whole becomes tender, add the soybeans (photo 2) and cover with the soaking water and dashi stock.
5. Combine the shoyu, sugar and sake and add (photo 3). Stirring off and on, simmer over medium heat until the liquid is absorbed.

Soybeans Dressed with Mayonnaise

Ingredients (4 servings)

2 cups boiled soybeans	3 Tbsp mayonnaise
some grated wasabi horse-radish	2 chives
	aojiso (green shiso leaves), radish, negi (Japanese leek)

[Calories 196 kcal., Protein 11.1 g]

Method: 1. Set aside the leaves of chives, and cut the remaining parts into pieces.
2. Add the wasabi and mayonnaise to the soybeans (photo), and mix. Combine the pieces of chives and mix lightly.
3. Spread the aojiso on a platter and place **2.** Garnish with wasabi, slices of radish and leaves of chives.

★ This recipe is prepared with ingredients at hand. The aromas of the wasabi and aojiso are superb.

Black Bean Rice

Deep-fried Edamame

Deep-fried Edamame

Ingredients (4 servings)

1 cup boiled edamame
  (young soybeans in pods)
3½ oz (100 g) prawns
½ bunch mitsuba
  (honewort)
1 small egg
½ cup ice water
1 cup pastry flour
Dipping Sauce
  { 2 Tbsp mirin
    ½ cup dashi stock
    2 Tbsp shoyu
salt, oil for deep-frying, lemon
[Calories 366 kcal., Protein 11.7 g]

Method: 1. Parboil the edamame according to page 13. Remove shells and peel off the thin outer skin (photo 1).
2. Devein prawns with a bamboo skewer. Cut the mitsuba into ¾″ (2 cm) lengths.
3. Combine the ingredients of dipping sauce in a saucepan and bring to a boil.
4. Beat the egg in a bowl and add the ice water. To make batter, add sieved flour and mix lightly. Dip edamame and prawns in the batter and mix lightly (photo 2).

5. Preheat the oil to 340°F (170°C). Drop **4** in the oil with two spoons (photo 3) and deep-fry. Serve with the dipping sauce and lemon cut into a wedge.

* * *

Black Bean Rice

Ingredients (4 servings)

1 cup boiled black beans
  (kuromame)
¾ oz (20 g) small shrimp
2 cups rice (1 cup = 200 cc)
2 Tbsp sake
[Calories 384 kcal., Protein 14.3 g]
1 Tbsp mirin
1 tsp shoyu
1 tsp salt
kaiware (white radish
    sprouts)

Method: 1. Wash the rice 30 minutes before cooking. Drain in a bamboo colander.
2. Place the rice in a cooker. Add water, all the ingredients except black beans, and cook.
3. When cooked, mix in black beans. Serve in a bowl topped with the kaiware.

★The combination of black beans and shrimp provides plenty of calcium.

JAPANESE-STYLE DISHES

Boiled Sauries

Steamed Rice with Soybeans

Steamed Rice with Soybeans

Ingredients (4 servings)

1 cup boiled soybeans
2 cups glutinous rice
   (1 cup = 200 cc)
4 pickled ume
1 Tbsp sake
10 aojiso (green shiso leaves)
toasted white sesame seeds
[Calories 370 kcal., Protein 11.7 g]

Method: 1. Wash the glutinous rice and drain in a bamboo colander.
2. Tear the flesh of pickled ume. Set aside the seeds for use. Cut the aojiso into julienne strips.
3. In a large heat-proof bowl, place the rice, 2 cups water, sake, ume flesh and seeds, and soybeans. Cover with plastic wrap and heat 12 minutes in a microwave oven. Allow it to steam another 7 ~8 minutes without removing the wrap.
4. Take off the wrap and mix all lightly. Serve in a bowl sprinkled with sesame seeds and aojiso.

Boiled Sauries

Ingredients (4 servings)

4 sauries
2 packs shimeji mushrooms
4~5 chives

Broth {
1 cup dashi stock
4 Tbsp shoyu
2 Tbsp sugar
2 Tbsp vinegar
1 Tbsp sake
1~2 tsp toubanjan (chili bean paste)
}

[Calories 331 kcal., Protein 19.8 g]

Method: 1. Cut off the head of the saury and cut into 2 portions. Remove the guts by inserting chopstick into the belly from the head side (photo 1). Wash well and pat dry. **2.** Cut away root clusters of the shimeji mushrooms and separate them. Cut the chives into 1

½″ (4 cm) lengths. **3.** Bring the broth to a boil in a saucepan. Add sauries and shimeji and cook over medium heat. Once in a while, ladle broth over (photo 2), and cook until it thickens. Serve in a bowl and garnish with chives.

★The shimeji and chives provide vitamins. The spicy toubanjan will stimulate your appetite.

Sweet Potato dressed with Vinegar

Tangle Shaving Soup

Sweet Potato Dressed with Vinegar

Ingredients (4 servings)

¼ momen-dofu (firm tofu)
½ sweet potato
½ head broccoli
salt

(A) {
1 Tbsp sesame paste (white)
2 tsp vinegar
1½ tsp sugar
½ salt
}

[Calories 86 kcal., Protein 4.1 g]

Method: 1. Drain the tofu according to page 4.
2. Cut the sweet potato with peel intact into ½″ (2 cm) cubes. Boil until tender and drain. Divide the broccoli into flowerets and boil in salted water and drain.
3. Mash the tofu in a mortar. Add (A) and mix until smoothed. Dress the sweet potato and broccoli lightly and serve in a bowl.

Tangle Shaving Soup

Ingredients (4 servings)

½ oz (15 g) tangle shavings
2 Tbsp dried young sardines

4 pieces baked fu (dried wheat gluten)
shoyu

[Calories 9 kcal., Protein 1.7 g]

Method: 1. Soak the fu in water until soft.
2. Place equal portions of tangle shavings, sardines and fu in a bowl. Pour in boiled water and add a few drops of shoyu.

★Add ground sesame seeds or julienne aojiso (green shiso leaves), if desired.
★Simple and easy soup when other soups are not available. Tangle shavings easily absorb moisture, so preserve them in an airtight container.

11

Chili Con Carne

Ingredients (4 servings)

1 cup boiled soybeans	
7 oz (200 g) ground beef	
½ small onion	
1 clove garlic	
1 small carrot	(A)
3 strips bacon	
½ tsp cumin seeds	
2 Tbsp butter	
Minced parsley	

(A) {
8 oz (230 g) canned tomato
3 Tbsp tomato ketchup
1 bouillon cube
1 Tbsp sugar
½ tsp salt
½ tsp nutmeg
½ tsp paprika
½ tsp chili powder
}

[Calories 373 kcal., Protein 17.9 g]

Method: 1. Mince the onion and garlic. Cut the carrot into ⅜″ (1 cm) cubes and cut the bacon into ⅜″ (1 cm) widths.

2. Heat the butter in a pan and stir-fry the onion and garlic over medium heat until browned (photo 1).

3. Add the cumin seeds and ground beef (photo 2) and continue stir-frying until broken into small pieces. Add the carrot and bacon.

4. Add 2 cups water, (A) and soybeans (photo 3) and cook over medium heat. When it comes to a boil, skim the surface to remove foam (photo 4). Lower the heat and cook for 20~30 minutes. Serve in a container and scatter minced parsley over.

★Cumin seeds are produced mainly in Iran and Turkey. The aromatic seeds have slightly bitter taste and they are used for curry and stew.

Mousse of Edamame

Ingredients (4 servings)

1½ cups edamame (young soybeans in pods)
1 cup soup
⅕ oz (5 g) powdered gelatin
2 Tbsp white wine
½ cup fresh cream
pinch pepper
salt, cherry tomatoes, basil, French bread

[Calories 202 kcal., Protein 8.8 g]

Method: 1. Add the gelatin to white wine. Boil the edamame in salted water as directed in **1** in the following recipe and shell.
2. Break down the edamame and soup in a blender to obtain thick liquid. Transfer to a pan and cook over low heat, stirring, continually. Add the gelatin and remove from the heat. Let it cool in a bowl.
3. Beat the fresh cream lightly. Add a pinch of salt and pepper. Mix in **2** (photo). Place in a container moistened by water and chill in the refrigerator.
4. Scoop with a spoon and serve in a platter with the cherry tomato, basil and French bread.

Marinated Octopus & Edamame

Ingredients (4 servings)

1 cup edamame (young soybeans in pods)
3½ oz (100 g) octopus leg
½ pack kaiware (white radish sprouts)
salt, hojiso (buds of young shiso leaves),
petals of chrysanthemum flowers, beni-tade (red water pepper)
Marinade
{ 3 Tbsp olive oil
1 Tbsp lemon juice
1 tsp mustard seeds
½ salt
pinch pepper }

[Calories 179 kcal., Protein 11.1 g]

Method: 1. Wash the edamame and rub with salt. Boil in plenty of hot water until soft and drain in a bamboo colander. Remove from the pod and peel off the thin skin.
2. Cut the octopus into thin slices.
3. Combine the ingredients of marinade. Add the edamame and octopus. Let it stand for some time until well seasoned. Serve in a container topped with the kaiware, hojiso, chrysanthemum petals, and beni-tade.

★The octopus and squid contain taurine which is good for eyes.

Marinated Octopus & Edamame

Mousse of Edamame

Curry Samosa

Ingredients (4 servings)

1 cup boiled soybeans	1 Tbsp curry powder
3½ oz (100 g) ground beef	4 egg roll wrappers
	1 Tbsp butter
½ small onion	some pastry flour
1 tsp cumin seeds	oil for frying, mint

[Calories 272 kcal., Protein 12.3 g]

Method: 1. Grind the soybeans with a food processor (photo 1). Mince the onion.
2. Melt the butter in a frying pan and stir-fry the onion and cumin seeds. Add the ground beef and soybeans. When they are broken into pieces, sprinkle with curry powder (photo 2) and mix all.
3. Quarter the egg roll wrapper. Place **2** on it. Dissolve the flour in a bit of water. Put the dissolved flour on the edges of the wrapper and fold it into a triangle (photo 3). Preheat the oil to 360°F (180°C) and deep-fry until browned. Serve in a platter with the mint.

Black Beans & Cucumber Salad

Ingredients (4 servings)

1 cup boiled black beans	Dressing
2 cucumbers	4 Tbsp olive oil
3½ oz (100 g) button mushrooms	2 Tbsp plain yogurt
	juice of 1 lemon
juice of ½ lemon	½ tsp salt
mint, grains of pepper (red)	pinch pepper

[Calories 197 kcal., Protein 7.5 g]

Method: 1. Cut the cucumber diagonally into ⅛″ (3 mm) thick slices. Remove stems of button mushrooms and cut into ¼″ (5 mm) thick slices. Pour the lemon juice over to prevent changing the color.
2. Make the dressing. Combine all the ingredients except the olive oil in a bowl and mix well. Add the olive oil little by little and mix all.
3. Arrange **1**, black beans and mint in a platter attractively. Scatter the grains of pepper and pour the dressing over.

Bean Hamburger

Ingredients (4 servings)

2 cups boiled soybeans
7 oz (200 g) ground beef
¼ onion
1 green pepper
1 clove garlic
1 tsp salt
pinch pepper
2 Tbsp pastry flour

2 Tbsp oil

(A)
{
1½ Tbsp salsa sauce
  (store bought)
1½ Tbsp tomato
  ketchup
1 tsp oyster sauce
pinch sugar
}

lettuce, lemon

[Calories 373 kcal., Protein 20.8 g]

Method: 1. Place the soybeans in a bowl and mash with a fork (photo 1).

2. Mince the onion, green pepper and garlic.

3. Combine the soybeans, ground beef, **2**, salt and pepper in a bowl (photo 2), mix until the meat becomes sticky. Divide into 8 portions and shape each into plump patty. Coat with flour.

4. Heat the oil in a frying pan. Place **3** and fry both sides over high heat (photo 3). Lower the heat to medium until well done.

5. Spread the lettuce leaf on a platter and place **4**. Serve with the lemon cut into a wedge. Make sauce by mixing the ingredients of (A) and pour over.

★The salsa sauce is a hot sauce. If you desire a milder taste, use 1½ Tbsp tomato ketchup in place of salsa sauce.

Prepared from Soybeans

WESTERN-STYLE DISHES

Abura-age Salad

Braised Tomato Rolls

Ingredients (4 servings)

1 cup boiled soybeans
3 eggs
9 oz (250 g) sliced beef
½ onion
1 clove garlic
2 Tbsp fresh cream
pinch nutmeg

(A) {
1 cup soup stock
3 Tbsp sauce for pizza
1 cup tomato sauce
1 bay leaf
}

pastry flour, salt, pepper, butter, minced parsley, powdered cheese

[Calories 423 kcal., Protein 24.1 g]

Method: 1. Chop the soybeans roughly into pieces. Mince the onion and garlic.
2. Beat eggs in a bowl. Add a pinch of salt and pepper and mix. Melt 2 Tbsp butter in a frying pan and pour in the egg mixture. Mix well with chopsticks and make soft scrambled eggs.
3. Combine the soybeans, scrambled eggs, 1 Tbsp flour, fresh cream, a pinch of salt and pepper and nutmeg in a bowl and mix well.
4. Arrange ¼ of the sliced beef on top of one another lengthwise and sprinkle with a pinch of salt, pepper and flour. Place ¼ of **3** in the front slice (photo 1), tuck in both edges and roll up. Make another three rolls in the same way.
5. Heat 1 Tbsp butter in a pan and stir-fry the onion and garlic over medium heat (photo 2). When softened, add (A).
6. As soon as it comes to a boil, add **4** (photo 3),

lower the heat and simmer for 15~20 minutes. Serve on a plate together with the sauce, and sprinkle with the parsley and powdered cheese.

★If you chop the soybeans coarsely, you can enjoy a simple taste.

Daikon & Scallop Soup

Braised Tomato Rolls

Abura-age Salad

Ingredients (4 servings)

2 pieces abura-age (deep-fried tofu)
14 oz (400 g) daikon (white radish)
2 tomatoes
½ onion
¾ oz (20 g) scallions

10 aojiso (green shiso leaves)
1¾ oz (50 g) canned tuna
(A) {
3 Tbsp mentsuyu (sauce for noodles) (store bought)
2~3 Tbsp vinegar
2 Tbsp sesame oil
}

[Calories 162 kcal., Protein 7.9 g]

Method: 1. Bake the abura-age in a toaster oven until browned. Cut in half and then cut into julienne strips.
2. Cut the daikon into thin strips, 1¼″ (3 cm) long. Cut the tomato into bite-sized pieces. Cut the onion into thin slices, soak in water and drain. Cut the scallion into pieces and aojiso into julienne strips. Drain tuna lightly.
3. Mix 3 Tbsp water and (A). Dress the ingredients and serve on a plate.

Daikon & Scallop Soup

Ingredients (4 servings)

7 oz (200 g) daikon (white radish)
2¾ oz (80 g) canned scallop

1 Tbsp cornstarch
(A) {
1 bouillon cube
1 Tbsp sake
}
leaves of daikon

[Calories 38 kcal., Protein 3.4 g]

Method: 1. Cut the daikon into julienne strips, 1¼″ (3 cm) long. **2.** Combine the liquid of the scallop can, 3 cups water and (A) in a saucepan, bring to a boil and cook the daikon until tender. Add the scallop broken up and the cornstarch dissolved in 2 Tbsp water. **3.** Serve in a bowl topped with boiled and minced daikon leaves.

Egg Rolls of Green
Soybeans & Bean Sprouts

Simmered Soybeans & Horse Mackerel

Ingredients (4 servings)

1 cup boiled soybeans
4 horse mackerels
1 naganegi (Japanese leek)
1 piece ginger
2 8″ (20 cm) square kombu
  (kelp)

1~2 red chili pepper
(A) {
½ cup vinegar
3 Tbsp shoyu
3 Tbsp sake
1 Tbsp sugar
3 Tbsp sesame oil
}

[Calories 343 kcal., Protein 24.0 g]

Method: 1. Scale the fish and pull out the gill from the gill cover (photo 1). Insert chopsticks into the gill cover, pick up the entrails (photo 2) and pull them out, twisting chopsticks (photo 3). Remove the remaining entrails with fingers. Wash in water and wipe dry. Make two incisions on the surface to be served with a knife.
2. Cut the naganegi into 2″ (5 cm) lengths. Slice the ginger. Cut the kombu into ¾″ (2 cm) square and soak in ½ cup water for 10~15 minutes. Set the water aside.

Soybeans & Drumstick Soup

Simmered Soybeans & Horse Mackerel

Egg Rolls of Green Soybeans & Bean Sprouts

Ingredients (4 servings)

1 cup boiled green soybeans	8 egg roll wrappers
1 pack soybean sprouts	some pastry flour
3 slices pork ham	1 Tbsp sesame oil
2 eggs	oil for frying
pinch salt, pepper	

[Calories 377 kcal., Protein 14.7 g]

Method: 1. Mash beans coarsely with a fork. Remove the root hair of bean sprouts. Cut the ham into julienne strips.
2. Heat the sesame oil in a frying pan. Stir-fry the bean sprouts and ham and season with salt and pepper. Add beaten egg and stir-fry until fluffy. Add soybeans and mix.
3. Divide **2** into 8 portions, and place each on the egg roll wrapper. Fold forward, tuck both edges in and roll up. Fix the end by the flour dissolved in a pinch of water. Preheat oil to 360°F (180°C) and deep-fry until browned.

Soybeans & Drumstick Soup

Ingredients (4 servings)

1½ cups boiled soybeans	¾ oz (20 g) string beans
8 drumsticks	1 bouillon cube
⅓ carrot	½ cup sake
1¾ oz (50 g) boiled bamboo shoots	pinch salt, pepper
⅕ oz (5 g) kikurage (cloud ear mushrooms)	½ tsp toubanjan (chili bean paste)

[Calories 255 kcal., Protein 18.3 g]

Method: 1. Soak the kikurage in water. Cut the larger ones in half. Cut the carrot and bamboo shoots into 2" (5 cm) long slices and cut diagonally in half.
2. Parboil the string beans and cut diagonally.
3. Wash the drumsticks, parboil in boiling water (photo) and drain.
4. Place the drumsticks, bouillon cube, sake and 6 cups water in a saucepan and cook over a high heat. When boiled, lower the heat and simmer for 20 minutes, skimming the surface to remove foam.
5. Add the soybeans and **1** and continue simmering until the carrot becomes tender. Season with salt and pepper and add the toubanjan.
6. Serve in a bowl topped with string beans.

3. Arrange the naganegi and kombu in a saucepan and place the fish on them. Add the ginger and chili pepper (photo 4). Pour in (A) and the water in which the kombu soaked and cook over medium heat. When it comes to a boil, add the soybeans (photo 5) and lower the heat and simmer for 20 minutes.

★The method of pulling the entrails out is used to keep the shape of the fish. You may remove the entrails by cutting the belly.

Stir-fried Black Beans & Squid

Ingredients (4 servings)

1 cup boiled black beans
1 squid
Seasoning

{ juice of 1 piece of ginger
1 tsp sake
pinch salt }

1 bunch nira (a type of leek)
¾ oz (20 g) naganegi (Japanese leek)
⅓ tsp toubanjan (chili bean paste)

pinch salt, pepper
3 Tbsp sesame oil

(A) {
1 piece ginger
3 Tbsp tomato ketchup
1 Tbsp sugar
1 Tbsp vinegar
1 Tbsp sake
½ Tbsp cornstarch
1 tsp Chinese soup mix (granule)
}

[Calories 237 kcal., Protein 15.0 g]

Method: 1. Pull the entrails out of the squid (photo 1) and skin. Cut the body into bite-sized pieces and make 2 or 3 incisions (photo 2). Chop the legs. Soak all in the seasoning.
2. Cut the nira into pieces, 1¼″ (3 cm) long. Mince the naganegi and the ginger in (A).
3. Drain the squid and stir-fry quickly in 1 Tbsp sesame oil.
4. Heat 2 Tbsp sesame oil in a pan and stir-fry the toubanjan and naganegi. Combine (A) and add (photo 3). Cook a while.
5. Add the nira and stir-fry and then add the squid. Add the black beans (photo 4), stir-fry lightly and season with salt and pepper. Serve on a plate.

Clean the Inside of Blood Vessels and Beat Adult Diseases

As we advance in age, we come to worry about high blood pressure, hardening of the arteries and myocardial infarction. All these diseases are related to blood vessels. Common with aging, cholesterol and lipids form on the inner arterial walls, making them thick and nonelastic and narrowing the opening of the vessel, causing high blood pressure. Hypertension develops atherosclerosis and induces various degenerative diseases such as apoplexy, angina pectoris, myocardial infarction, cerebral infarction and renal failure.

It is said that the vessel grows old with age. Plenty of nutrients which are essential to keep the vessel young are contained in soybeans. One of them is high quality protein. Protein keeps the vessel strong and elastic. Lecithin and saponin wash away the extra cholesterol accumulated in the vessel and excrete it from the body. Fermented soybeans (natto) have a powerful enzyme which dissolves blood clots.

It is well known that salt raises blood pressure. The potassium in soybeans plays a role in checking the raise. But you should be careful not to use too much salt in cooking. Those who are not accustomed to lightly-flavored food should use vinegar, spices and herbs.

Another matter which worries us when we grow old is the aging of the brain. In this regard, soybeans are a great help. The lecithin in soybeans is a very important component of the membrane of the brain's nerve cell. If you take sufficient lecithin, the nerve cell functions properly. Lack of lecithin causes trouble in transmitting signals to the brain. Choline, one of the components of lecithin, is an ingredient of acetylcholine, which is essential for the conduction of nerve impulses, and it is said to affect memory and concentration.

No wonder elderly people are fond of soybeans and tofu. Eat soybeans as much as possible to prolong youth.

Prepared from Soybeans
CHINESE-STYLE DISHES

Tomato Salad
with Young Sardines

String Beans
with Sesame Sauce

Tofu & Pickled
Ume Soup

Minced Soybeans
on Lettuce

Minced Soybeans on Lettuce

Ingredients (4 servings)
1 cup boiled soybeans	⎧ 1 cup Chinese soup
7 oz (200 g) ground pork	⎪ 3 Tbsp shoyu
1 clove garlic	(A) ⎨ 2 Tbsp sake
⅓ piece ginger	⎪ 2 Tbsp vinegar
6″ (15 cm) naganegi	⎩ 1½ Tbsp sugar
(Japanese leek)	½ Tbsp cornstarch
1 red chili pepper	1 Tbsp sesame oil
1 head lettuce	mitsuba (honewort)
1 carrot	

[Calories 286 kcal., Protein 17.0 g]

Method: 1. Mince the soybeans coarsely with a knife. Mince the garlic, ginger and naganegi. Soften the chili pepper in water, seed and cut into pieces.

Remove the core of the lettuce and cut into 1½″ (4 cm) cubes. Cut the carrot into julienne strips, 1¼″ (3 cm) long.

2. Heat the sesame oil in a pan, and stir-fry the garlic, ginger and naganegi. Add the chili pepper, break up the pork and continue frying. Add the soybeans (photo 1), mix well (A) and cook for 7~8 minutes (photo 2).

3. Add the cornstarch dissolved in 1 Tbsp water. Serve on a plate over the lettuce, carrot and mitsuba.

Tofu & Pickled Ume Soup

Ingredients (4 servings)
1 block kinugoshi-dofu	4~5 chives
(silken tofu)	3 cups Chinese soup
2 umeboshi (pickled	1 Tbsp sake
ume)	1 Tbsp cornstarch
2 cloves garlic	2 Tbsp sesame oil
1 piece ginger	

[Calories 120 kcal., Protein 4.2 g]

Method: 1. Seed the umeboshi and break up the flesh. Mince the garlic and ginger. Chop the chives finely.

2. Heat the sesame oil in a pan and stir-fry the garlic and ginger over medium flame. When the aroma is full, add the tofu, breaking up by hand (photo). Lightly stir-fry until the whole is covered with oil. Add the ume, soup and sake and bring to a boil.

3. Add the cornstarch dissolved in 2 Tbsp water to thicken. Serve in a bowl topped with the chives.

Tomato Salad with Young Sardines

Ingredients (4 servings)
2 tomatoes	Dressing
8 aojiso (green shiso leaves)	⎧ 2 Tbsp mentsuyu
2 Tbsp chirimenjako	⎪ (soup for noodles)
(dried young sardines)	⎨ (store bought)
2 tsp sesame oil	⎪ 1 Tbsp vinegar
	⎩ ½ Tbsp sesame oil

[Calories 73 kcal., Protein 4.6 g]

Method: 1. Cut tomatoes into 6 to 8 wedges. Cut the aojiso into julienne strips.

2. Heat the sesame oil in a pan and stir-fry sardines until crispy (photo).

3. Combine the ingredients of dressing and mix well.

4. Serve tomatoes on a plate topped with sardines and aojiso. Pour the dressing over.

★Sardines provide calcium and aojiso vitamin A.

String Beans with Sesame Sauce

Ingredients (4 servings)
7 oz (200 g) string beans	salt
2 Tbsp toasted white ses-	(A) ⎧ 2 Tbsp mayonnaise
ame seeds	⎩ ½ Tbsp shoyu

[Calories 88 kcal., Protein 2.7 g]

Method: 1. Parboil string beans in salted water and drain. Cut diagonally into 1½″ (4 cm) lengths.

2. Grind sesame seeds until sticky. Add (A) and mix well. Add string beans and mix lightly and serve in a bowl.

★Sesame seeds contain plenty of calcium, iron and vitamin B_1.

Chapter 2

TOFU & NATTO DISHES

Among the processed foods of soybeans, typical examples are tofu and natto. The plain taste of tofu is used in various dishes. When heated, natto gives a different delicious taste. Koori-dofu (freeze-dried tofu) and okara (tofu lees) are utilized for making cake.

Japanese-style Tofu Steak

Ingredients (4 servings)

4 blocks momen-dofu (firm tofu)
1 pack shimeji mushrooms
4 fresh shiitake mushrooms
{ 7 oz (200 g) daikon radish
2~3 red chili peppers

2 chives
4 Tbsp pastry flour
4 Tbsp sesame oil
1¾ oz (50 g) daikon radish
¾ oz (20 g) carrot
salt, pepper, ito-tougarashi (thin chili pepper), shoyu

[Calories 394 kcal., Protein 22.8 g]

Method: 1. Drain the tofu as directed on page 4.
2. Cut away root clusters of the shimeji and separate them. Remove stems from shiitake and cut caps into slices. Chop the chives finely. Cut the daikon and carrot into julienne strips for garnish.
3. Soak and soften red chili peppers in water and seed. Pare the daikon and make 2 or 3 holes with a chopstick. Insert red chili peppers in the holes and grate (photo 1). Drain lightly.
4. Heat the sesame oil in a frying pan and stir-fry the shimeji and shiitake (photo 2). Sprinkle with pinch salt and pepper and remove.
5. Cut the tofu in half sideways and lightly season with salt and pepper. Cover the whole with flour. Heat 3 Tbsp sesame oil in a frying pan and brown both sides of tofu, continually moving the pan (photo 3).
6. Place the tofu on a plate and top with **3**. Add mushrooms, daikon and carrot. Scatter chives and ito-tougarashi over all. Season with shoyu.

TOFU: There are two kinds; dehydrated 'momen-dofu' (firm tofu) and watery 'kinu-goshi-dofu' (silken tofu). Can be stored in the refrigerator for one or two days.

KOORI-DOFU: Made by freezing tofu, thawing and squeezing out excess water. It is then dried. It is also called 'kouya-dofu' and 'shimi-dofu'.

NATTO: Fermented soybeans. It is easy to digest and assimilate. Contains various vitamins.

OKARA: Lees of tofu. Contains plenty of dietary fiber. It is also called 'u-no-hana'.

Cherry Tomatoes with Tofu

Grated Natto & Noodles

Grated Natto & Noodles

Ingredients (4 servings)

14 oz (400 g) soba
  (dried buckwheat noodles)
4 packs natto
7 oz (200 g) daikon radish
8 okra
toasted nori, citron peel,

grated wasabi horseradish
Sauce
  ⎰ 1 cup dashi stock
  ⎱ 6 Tbsp shoyu
     4 Tbsp mirin

[Calories 467 kcal., Protein 22.9 g]

Method: 1. Grate the daikon and squeeze the juice out. Parboil the okra, drain and cut into thin round slices. Cut the nori and citron peel into julienne strips.
2. Combine the ingredients of sauce in a saucepan and bring to a boil. Let it stand to cool.
3. Boil the soba noodles according to the directions on the package. Soak in cold water and drain in a bamboo colander.
4. Serve the soba on a plate topped with **1**, natto and wasabi. Pour the sauce over.

★Natto and soba noodles have ample vitamins. Grated radish and okra promote the digestion.
★You may use store-bought sauce if available.

Cherry Tomatoes with Tofu

Ingredients (4 servings)

½ block momen-dofu
  (firm tofu)
1 pack cherry tomatoes
2 Tbsp white sesame seeds

1 Tbsp sugar
⅓ tsp salt
½ tsp shoyu
watercress

[Calories 91 kcal., Protein 4.5 g]

Method: 1. Drain the tofu as directed on page 4.
2. Parboil cherry tomatoes and transfer to cold water. Skin and remove the calyx.
3. Grind sesame seeds until sticky. Add the tofu, sugar, salt and shoyu (photo) and mix well until smooth.
4. Dress tomatoes with **3** and serve in a bowl. Top with the watercress.

★For this dish, the momen-dofu (firm tofu) is preferable to the kinugoshi-dofu (silken tofu), since the former is less watery.

Okara with Littleneck Clam

Ingredients (4 servings)

10 5/8 oz (300 g) okara (tofu lees)

7 oz (200 g) shucked littleneck clam

1/5 oz (5 g) dried shiitake mushrooms

1 3/4 oz (50 g) gobou (burdock root)

1 3/4 oz (50 g) lotus root

1 3/4 oz (50 g) carrot

2 3/4 oz (80 g) naganegi (Japanese leek)

1 egg

some dashi stock

2 Tbsp sake

3 Tbsp sugar

4 Tbsp shoyu

4 Tbsp oil

vinegar, salt, chives

[Calories 314 kcal., Protein 12.1 g]

Method: 1. Soak shiitake mushrooms in just enough water to cover. Remove the stems and cut into thin slices. Reserve the soaking water. Shave the gobou and cut the lotus root into quarter-rounds. Soak both in vinegared water and drain. Mince the carrot and cut the naganegi into thin round slices.
2. Rinse the clams in lightly salted water and drain. Sprinkle with sake and stir-fry over high heat. Transfer to a bamboo colander placed in a bowl. Reserve the liquid.
3. Heat 2 Tbsp oil in a saucepan and stir-fry all the ingredients except naganegi. Add 2 Tbsp oil and the okara and continue stir-frying, taking care not to burn.
4. Make 2 1/2 cups sauce with the dashi stock, shiitake-soaked water and clam liquid. Add the sugar and shoyu (photo) and cook, stirring, until the liquid has evaporated. Add the clams, beaten egg and mix quickly. Add the naganegi and turn off the heat. Serve in a bowl topped with the chives chopped finely.

Ground Koori-dofu

Ingredients (4 servings)

4 koori-dofu (freeze-dried tofu)

3 1/2 oz (100 g) ground chicken

aonori laver

Sauce

2 cups dashi stock

3 Tbsp shoyu

2 Tbsp sugar

2 Tbsp mirin

[Calories 183 kcal., Protein 13.0 g]

Method: 1. Grind the koori-dofu and soften by pouring on boiling water (photo). Change boiling water and transfer to a dish towel spread in a bamboo colander. Wring the towel and squeeze out water.
2. Bring the sauce to a boil in a saucepan. Add the ground chicken and cook, stirring until it crumbles to pieces.
3. Add the koori-dofu and cook over low heat until the liquid has evaporated. Serve in a bowl and top with the aonori laver.

Good for Serving Guests **CANAPE-STYLE CHILLED TOFU**

If you try a new type of condiments, the usual chilled tofu turns to an attractive dish. Cut the tofu into bite-sized pieces and hollow out the surface to insert condiments.

●Kimchi & Peanuts

Mince the kimchi (Korean pickles) and drain. Combine with minced peanuts and place on the tofu. The spicy taste of kimchi goes well with that of savory peanuts.

●Myouga & Pickled Ume

Cut the myouga (Japanese ginger) into thin sticks. Seed the pickled ume and pound the flesh with a knife. Place on the tofu and top with toasted white sesame seeds.

●Mentaiko & Okra

Rub the okra with salt, boil in hot water and drain. Pound to pieces with a knife. Make an incision on the skin of mentaiko (salted ovary of pollack) and draw out the contents. Place the okra on the tofu and top with the mentaiko.

●Natto & Aojiso

Cut the aojiso (green shiso leaves) in half and then into julienne strips. Place the aojiso on the tofu and top with the natto.

●Mountain Yam & Chives

Skin the mountain yam and grate. Place on the tofu and garnish with the chives.

● **Chirimenjako & Shishitou**

Cut the shishitou (small green pepper) into thin round slices. Heat a dash of oil in a frying pan and stir-fry the shishitou and chirimenjako (dried young sardines) until crispy. Place on the tofu.

● **Zhasai & Bacon**

Mince the zhasai (pickled mustard tuber) and bacon. Heat a dash of oil in a frying pan and fry the bacon until crispy. Place together with the zhasai on the tofu.

● **Cucumber & Neriuni**

Cut the cucumber in thin slices and soften by sprinkling with salt. Squeeze out water and place on the tofu. Top generously with the neriuni (sea urchin paste).

Soybeans make Bones Strong and Prevent Colon Cancer

Calcium is a principal element of bones. About 99 percent of the calcium is found in bones and teeth, and the remaining 1 percent in blood. If there is a deficit of calcium, the calcium in bones dissolves in blood to make up for the lack, and the shortfall in calcium makes bones fragile, developing osteoporosis. Calcium is a very important nutrient for growing children as well as for adults.

As main sources of calcium, milk and small fish are well known, but it is amply contained in soybeans and processed foods such as koori-dofu (freeze-dried tofu) and abura-age (deep-fried tofu). Soybeans also contain a substance which prevents the outflow of calcium from bones. Natto (fermented soybeans) has vitamin K_2, which makes bones strong.

One of other important nutrients of soybeans is dietary fiber. The deficit of fiber causes foods to remain in colon overly long, which is responsible for developing cancer. In other words, dietary fiber is essential for the prevention of colon cancer. Among processed foods, okara (tofu lees), natto and kinako (soybeans flour) are outstanding in the content of dietary fiber. We should think better of traditional Japanese foods and try to eat them daily.

Toasted Tofu & Mushrooms

Ingredients (4 servings)

2 blocks toasted tofu
1 pack shimeji mushrooms
3½ oz (100 g) fresh shiitake mushrooms
2¾ oz (80 g) enokidake mushrooms

2 cups dashi stock
1 Tbsp shoyu
2 Tbsp mirin
½ tsp salt
1 Tbsp cornstarch
Mitsuba (honewort)

[Calories 165 kcal., Protein 13.8 g]

Method: 1. Cut each block of toasted tofu into 6 portions.
2. Cut away root clusters of the shimeji, and separate. Remove stems of shiitake and cut caps into slices. Cut away roots of enokidake and cut in half.
3. Heat the dashi stock in a saucepan and cook mushrooms. When it comes to a boil, lower the heat, and season with shoyu, mirin and salt.
4. Add the tofu and add the cornstarch dissolved in 1 Tbsp water to thicken (photo).
5. Serve on a plate and scatter the mitsuba cut into 1¼″ (3 cm) lengths.

Natto Soup

Ingredients (4 servings)

2½ packs natto (fermented soybeans)
4 taros
½ pack shimeji mushrooms

3 cups dashi stock
3 Tbsp miso (soybean paste)
mitsuba (honewort)

[Calories 93 kcal., Protein 6.8 g]

Method: 1. Cut away root clusters of the shimeji, and separate. Pare taros and cut into bite-sized pieces.
2. Bring the dashi stock to a boil and cook the shimeji and taros. When it comes to a boil, lower the heat, and simmer until taros become tender. Stir in the miso (photo).
3. Add the natto and mitsuba cut into big pieces. Turn off the heat.

★The sticky substance of the taro and natto is called mucin and it promotes the digestion.

Braised Koori-dofu

Ingredients (4 servings)

2 pieces koori-dofu (freeze-dried tofu)
2¾ oz (80 g) prawns
⅛ oz (4 g) dried wakame seaweed
some cornstarch
oil for frying, citron peel,

mitsuba (honewort)
Sauce
⎰ 3 cups dashi stock
⎮ 1 Tbsp shoyu
⎮ 1 Tbsp mirin
⎱ ½ tsp salt

[Calories 115 kcal., Protein 7.2 g]

Method: 1. Reconstitute the koori-dofu as directed on page 5. Cut into bite-sized pieces. Dust the whole with cornstarch. Preheat oil to 320°F (160°C) and deep-fry until colored (photo).
2. Devein prawns. Soak the wakame in water and soften. Cut into big pieces.
3. Bring the sauce to a boil in a saucepan and add **1** and **2**. When prawns are cooked, transfer to a bowl. Garnish with the mitsuba cut into 1½″ (4 cm) lengths and minced citron peel.

Tofu & Cod Roe

Ingredients (4 servings)

1½ blocks kinugoshi-dofu (silken tofu)
2 oz (60 g) cod roe
⅓ cup boiled edamame (young soybeans in pods)
1 tsp cornstarch

salt
Sauce
⎰ 1 cup dashi stock
⎮ 2 Tbsp sake
⎮ 2 tsp shoyu
⎱ pinch salt

[Calories 113 kcal., Protein 10.8 g]

Method: 1. Cut the tofu in half sideways. Cut into a flower shape with a cutter.
2. Cut the cod roe in half. Make an incision lengthwise and draw out the contents. Parboil the edamame in salted water as directed on page 13. Shell and remove the thin skin.
3. Bring the sauce to a boil in a saucepan and add the tofu, cod roe and edamame (photo). When the tofu is heated, stir in the cornstarch dissolved in 2 tsp water to thicken.

Yu-dofu
(simmered tofu)

Ingredients (4 servings)

2 blocks kinugoshi-dofu (silken tofu)
1 sheet kombu kelp (6″ (15 cm) square)
3½ oz (100 g) chicken breast
Seasoning { 1 Tbsp sake
pinch salt
walnuts, citron peel, chives, nametake mushrooms (bottled, storebought), toasted white sesame seeds, shoyu
[Calories 196 kcal., Protein 13.6 g]

Method: 1. Place the kombu kelp and water in an earthenware pot. Let stand for 10~15 minutes. **2.** Place the chicken in a heat-proof plate and season with sake and salt (photo). Place in a preheated steamer and steam over medium heat 15 minutes. When it cools, tear into thin pieces. **3.** Cut the tofu into chunks. Chop walnuts coarsely and cut citron peel into julienne strips. Cut chives into thin round slices. Mix name-take and sesame seeds. **4.** Place the tofu in an earthenware pot and simmer over medium heat. Add condiments you like to shoyu and dip the tofu when eating.

* * *

Yu-dofu

Natto & Fried Leaf Mustard

Ingredients (4 servings)

2 packs natto
5¼ oz (150 g) pickled leaf mustard
5¼ oz (150 g) slices of boned ribs of pork
[Calories 249 kcal., Protein 14.9 g]

4″ (10 cm) naganegi (Japanese leek)
1 red chili pepper
1 Tbsp sake
1 tsp shoyu
1 Tbsp sesame oil

Method: 1. Rinse the leaf mustard in water to remove salt. Squeeze out water and cut into pieces, ⅜″ (1 cm) long. Cut the pork slices into bite-sized pieces. Soften the chili pepper in water and seed. Cut the pepper and naganegi together into thin round slices. **2.** Heat the sesame oil in a pan, stir-fry the naganegi and chili pepper until the aroma comes out. Add the pork. **3.** When pork color changes white, stir in leaf mustard and natto. Season with sake and shoyu.

Natto & Fried Leaf Mustard

Shrimp & Egg Custard

Ingredients (4 servings)

1 block kinugoshi-dofu (silken tofu)
3½ oz (100 g) shelled shrimp
1¾ oz (50 g) carrot
¾ oz (20 g) snow peas

(A) {
1 egg
1 Tbsp cornstarch
½ tsp sugar
½ tsp salt
}

(B) {
½ cup dashi stock
½ Tbsp mirin
½ Tbsp shoyu
½ Tbsp sake
pinch salt
}

dash sake

½ Tbsp cornstarch
salt, mitsuba (honewort)

[Calories 120 kcal., Protein 9.5 g]

Method: 1. Drain the tofu as directed on page 4. Devein the shrimp and chop. Sprinkle with sake. Cut the carrot into julienne strips and boil. Parboil the snow peas in salted water and cut into thin strips.
2. Mix **1** and (A) (photo 1). Divide into 4 portions and place each on plastic wrap spread in a bowl. Squeeze the wrap into a bag (photo 2). Fasten the neck with a rubber band and cook in a microwave oven 6 minutes.
3. Combine ingredients (B) in a saucepan and bring to a boil. Add the cornstarch dissolved in 1 Tbsp water to thicken (photo 3).
4. Remove the wrap and serve in a bowl garnished with the mitsuba.

Shrimp & Egg Custard

Reproduce
TOFU HYAKUCHIN

"Tofu Hyakuchin" is a cookbook published in Edo-period (1600–1868). It lists a hundred methods of cooking tofu. Here are reproduced three recipes from the book. Let's enjoy the traditional simple taste.

34

Thunder Tofu

Ingredients (4 servings)

2 blocks momen-dofu (firm tofu)
3½ oz (100 g) daikon radish
4~5 scallions
3 Tbsp shoyu
3 Tbsp sesame oil
peppercorns

[Calories 217 kcal., Protein 11.2 g]

Method: 1. Drain the tofu as directed on page 4.
2. Grate the daikon and lightly squeeze out the juice. Cut the scallion into thin round slices.
3. Heat the sesame oil in a pan. Crumble the tofu into the pan over high heat. When the whole gets oily, pour the shoyu around the pan and stir-fry quickly.
4. Serve on a plate topped with **2**. Sprinkle with ground peppercorns.

Clear Tofu

Ingredients (4 servings)

½ block kinugoshi-dofu (silken tofu)
½ stick (5″ (13 cm)) agar
mustard, shoyu

[Calories 26 kcal., Protein 2.3 g]

Method: 1. Soak the agar in ample water for 30 minutes.
2. Cut the tofu in half sideways and then into 4 portions as you like.
3. Squeeze water out of the agar. Tear and place in a saucepan. Pour in 2 cups water and cook. When it comes to a boil, lower the heat, and simmer 5~6 minutes, stirring. Strain and let it cool.
4. Arrange the tofu in a moistened mold at intervals. Pour in the agar liquid gently. Chill in the refrigerator.
5. Cut and divide along the tofu. Serve on a plate and eat with mustard-shoyu mix.

★If molasses is used in place of mustard-shoyu mix, it will make a good desert.

Puffy Tofu

Ingredients (4 servings)

⅓ block kinugoshi-dofu (silken tofu)
4 eggs
2 cups dashi stock
peppercorns (white)

[Calories 111 kcal., Protein 8.7 g]

Method: 1. Place the tofu in a bowl and crumble with a whisk. Add beaten eggs (photo 1). Mix well until smooth.
2. Bring the dashi stock to a boil in an earthenware pot and add **1** (photo 2). Simmer, gently stirring. Turn off the heat and sprinkle with peppercorns ground coarsely. Take care not to cook too long or eggs will thicken. Eat as soon as cooked.

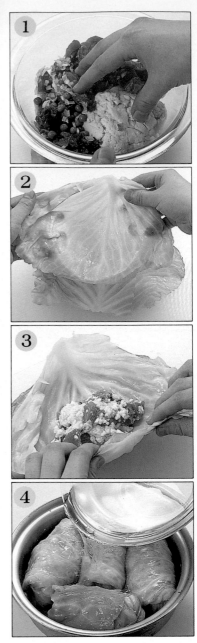

Tofu Stuffed Cabbage Rolls

Ingredients (4 servings)

1 block momen-dofu (firm tofu)
8 cabbage leaves
2 fresh salmon
⅛ oz (3 g) cloud ear mushrooms
¼ naganegi (Japanese leek)
¾ oz (20 g) green peas (frozen)

¼ onion
1 egg
(A) { 2 bouillon cubes
1 bay leaf
4 Tbsp tomato ketchup
1 Tbsp butter
salt, minced parsley

[Calories 249 kcal., Protein 20.0 g]

Method: 1. Drain the tofu as directed on page 4.
2. Skin and bone the salmon and cut into ⅜″ (1 cm) cubes. Reconstitute the cloud ear in water and cut into pieces. Mince the naganegi. Parboil the green peas and drain.

3. Parboil the cabbage in a generous amount of salted water. Spread in a bamboo colander and cool. Cut off large veins of each leaf. Reserve the boiling liquid.
4. Combine the tofu, **2** and egg and mix well (photo 1).
5. Spread 2 leaves flat so that the leaf end overlaps (photo 2). Place ¼ portions of **4**, roll up (photo 3) and fasten with a toothpick. Make 4 rolls in all.
6. Heat the butter in a deep saucepan and stir-fry the onion until transparent. Arrange **5** and pour in 3 cups water in which cabbage leaves boiled (photo 4). Add (A) and simmer over low heat 40~50 minutes. Serve on a plate and sprinkle with minced parsley.

Okara Soup

Ingredients (4 servings)

7 oz (200 g) okara (tofu lees)
5¼ oz (150 g) gobou (burdock root)
½ onion
2 slices bacon
2 Tbsp pastry flour

2 cups milk
2 bouillon cubes
2 Tbsp fresh cream
pinch salt, pepper
3 Tbsp butter
vinegar, minced parsley

[Calories 282 kcal., Protein 8.3 g]

Method: 1. Cut the gobou diagonally into 1¼″ (3 cm) lengths and then into thin strips. Soak in vinegared water and drain. Cut the onion in thin slices. Cut the bacon into pieces, ¼″ (5 mm) wide.
2. Heat the butter in a saucepan and stir-fry the onion and bacon until pliable. Add the gobou and continue stir-frying. Sprinkle in the pastry flour (photo 1).
3. When the flour is dissolved, pour in 1 cup water and milk (photo 2) and simmer over medium heat until it thickens. Add bouillon cubes, salt and pepper and simmer further 10~15 minutes.
4. Add the okara (photo 3) and simmer 4~5 minutes, stirring. Place on a plate. Add the cream and sprinkle with minced parsley.

Toasted Koori-dofu

Ingredients (4 servings)

4 piece koori-dofu (freeze-dried tofu)
Sauce
{ 3 cups dashi stock
2 Tbsp shoyu
1 Tbsp sugar
½ tsp mirin
½ tsp salt
1¾ oz (50 g) processed cheese

pinch pastry flour
1 egg
(A) { 1 cup breadcrumbs
4 Tbsp powdered cheese
4 Tbsp minced parsley
2 Tbsp oil
cherry tomatoes, parsley

[Calories 378 kcal., Protein 20.0 g]

Method: 1. Reconstitute the koori-dofu as on page 5. Cook in the boiling sauce. Drain and cut in half sideways. Make incisions and slice the cheese, ¼″ (8 mm) thick. Sandwich the cheese between the tofu. Coat with the pastry flour, egg and (A) in this order.
2. Spread aluminum foil on the tray in a toaster oven and arrange **1**. Pour over the oil and toast 15 minutes. Cut diagonally in half and serve on a plate. Garnish with cherry tomatoes and parsley.

Tofu &
Pine Nut Salad

Natto Pizza

Tofu & Pine Nut Salad

Ingredients (4 servings)

2 blocks kinugoshi-dofu
 (silken tofu)
1 tomato
3½ oz (100 g) daikon
 radish
⅓ carrot
1 cucumber
5 aojiso (green shiso leaves)

½ red onion
2 Tbsp pine nuts
Dressing
⎰ 2 Tbsp vinegar
⎰ ⅓ cup olive oil
⎱ 1 Tbsp chili sauce
⎱ ½ tsp salt
⎱ pinch pepper
1½ oz (45 g) potato chips

[Calories 352 kcal., Protein 10.0 g]

Method: 1. Drain the tofu as directed on page 4 and cut
into 6 portions.
2. Cut the tomato into wedges. Cut the daikon,
carrot, cucumber, and aojiso into thin strips. Cut the
onion into thin slices, soak in water and drain.
3. Make the dressing by combining all the ingredients except oil and mix. Add the oil little by little,
stirring.

4. Place the tofu and vegetables colorfully on a plate.
Add the pine nuts and crumbled potato chips and
pour the dressing over.

Natto Pizza

Ingredients (4 servings)

2 packs natto
 (with sauce and mustard)
¼ onion
20 pieces gyoza wrapper

2 oz (60 g) cheese for
 pizza
1 Tbsp butter
minced parsley

[Calories 211 kcal., Protein 10.1 g]

Method: 1. Mince onion and stir-fry in butter until transparent. Add natto with sauce and mustard and mix.
2. Divide **1** into 20 portions and place each on the
gyoza wrapper. Scatter the cheese over. Place on the
tray in a toaster oven and toast 5 minutes. Sprinkle
with minced parsley.

Soybeans are Good for Beauty and Figure

So far the topic has been focused on health, but now let's turn our eyes to other elements of soybeans. It is a wish of us to stay young as long as we live with beautiful skin, a lovely figure, and abundant hair. This dream will come true if we take good care to have a balanced diet.

First of all, it is important to take high quality protein and vitamin E to keep fresh and creamy skin. We have to take vitamins A and C to make vitamin E function effectively. Soybeans contain protein and vitamin E, but not vitamins A and C, so we have to eat vegetables which are full of vitamins A and C.

Soybeans and tofu are also good foods to go on a diet. Tofu has low calories and is easy to adapt to various dishes. If it is taken with rice, the nutritional combination is superb, because they make up for each deficit. Traditional Japanese dishes, therefore, are suited to maintain shapely figures.

Lastly, the essential condition for beautiful hair is to have a good circulation of blood. In China, hair is called 'excessive blood.' Thus blood is closely related to hair. As referred on page 21, soybeans clean blood vessels, so they are responsible for glossy, smooth and healthy hair. In other words, those healthy people who have clean blood vessels have young hair.

Let's make MOMEN-DOFU

Using the ingredients of your choice, you can make your own fresh tofu. Even if the shape is a little awkward, the taste will give you full satisfaction. It is worth giving it a try.

Ingredients (2 blocks)
2 cups soybeans 3 Tbsp nigari (bittern)

★ Nigari is a coagulant sold at natural food stores. It is also available from tofu shops. When using solid nigari, dissolve it in lukewarm water as directed.

●**Necessary utensils:** Blender or food processor, large saucepan, dish towel, thermometer, bamboo colander, large bowl, wooden spatula, chopsticks, and ladle.

1 Wash soybeans in water. Remove foreign particles and floating beans. Soak in 6 cups water overnight. (Store in the refrigerator in summer.)

A cross-section of well-soaked soybeans and insufficiently soaked soybeans. The former (left) is compact, but the latter (right) has a cavity, which means it needs further soaking for 2 ～3 hours.

2 Place ½ of drained soybeans in a blender and cover with the water in which they were soaked. Blend until smooth. In the same way, blend the remaining soybeans. This is called 'namago.'

3 Transfer **2** to a saucepan. Add 8 cups water. Rinse the soybeans out of the inside of the blender and add.

4 Cook over high heat, stirring from the bottom.

5 When it comes to a boil, lower heat to moderate and simmer 10～15 minutes, stirring. When soybeans are cooked, the raw smell disappears. This liquid is called 'go.'

6 Spread a dry kitchen towel over a bamboo colander placed in a bowl. Pour **5** over.

7 Using chop-sticks, wring the towel, twisting while hot. When it has cooled, wring further with hands.

The liquid thus obtained is soymilk. Fresh soymilk has a plenty of body and faint sweetness.

The lees which remained in the towel is 'okara.' This is high quality okara, so put it to good use.

8 Boil water in a large pan and warm the vessel containing the soymilk. Keep the temperature 160°F (70°C) ~ 165°F (75°C). If the temperature is too high, the tofu becomes solid, and if too low, it doesn't thichen properly.

9 Add 1½ Tbsp nigari by pouring it down a wooden spatula and stir gently.

10 Insert a thermometer and cover with a lid. Let it stand about 5 minutes, keeping the temperature between 160°F (70°C) ~ 165° F (75°C).

11 Gradually add the remaining nigari, stirring to the center, and judging as you go.

12 When the surface becomes transparent, it is unnecessary to add more nigari. If it is not transparent, add the remaining nigari and mix.

13 Spread a dish towel over a bamboo colander placed in a bowl. Transfer the cake of **12** into the towel. This is called 'oboro-dofu.' It is smooth and has a special taste only hand-made tofu has.

14 Wrap **13** in the towel, talking care not to crease. Place two plates as a weight and let stand 10~15 minutes.

15 Open the towel in water in a bowl. Leave the tofu in water until completely cooled to get rid of the smell of nigari.

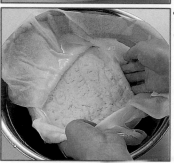

Drain lightly and serve on a plate. Top with the scallions cut into pieces and grated ginger. Pour shoyu over them.

Chili Sauce of Tofu & Shrimp

Ingredients (4 servings)

2 blocks momen-dofu (firm tofu)

5¼ oz (150 g) shelled shrimp

¾ oz (20 g) naganegi (Japanese leek)

1 piece ginger

1 clove garlic

5 scallions

½ Tbsp cornstarch

[Calories 306 kcal., Protein 16.3 g]

3 Tbsp sesame oil

(A)
- ½ cup Chinese soup
- ½ cup tomato ketchup
- 2 Tbsp sugar
- 2 Tbsp sake
- 1 tsp chili sauce
- ½ tsp salt
- pinch pepper

Method: 1. Drain the tofu as directed on page 4. Cut a block of tofu in half lenghwise and then into pieces, ½″ (1.5 cm) thick.

2. Devein the shrimp. Mince the naganegi, ginger and garlic. Cut scallions into ⅜″ (1 cm) lengths.

3. Heat the oil in a pan and stir-fry the naganegi, ginger and garlic (photo 1) until aromatic. Add the shrimp and continue stir-frying. Combine the ingredients of (A) and add (photo 2). Add the tofu (photo 3) and bring to a boil (photo 4).

4. Pour cornstarch dissolved in 1 Tbsp water over (photo 5) and thicken the whole.

5. Sprinkle with minced scallion and serve.

Natto Shaomai

Ingredients (30 pieces)

2 packs natto (fermented soybeans)
7 oz (200 g) ground pork
1 naganegi (Japanese leek)
¾ oz (20 g) corn (canned)
¾ oz (20 g) green peas (frozen)
2 fresh shiitake mushrooms

1½ oz (40 g) shelled shrimp
(A)
- ½ beaten egg
- 4 Tbsp cornstarch
- 1 Tbsp shoyu
- 1 tsp sugar
- 1 tsp salt
- 1 tsp sesame oil
30 shaomai (Chinese meat dumpling) wrappers

[Calories 313 kcal., Protein 17.2 g]

Method: 1. Mince the naganegi. Drain the corn. Remove the stem of shiitake and cut the cap into ¼″ (5 mm) cubes. Devein the shrimp and cut into ⅜″ (1 cm) cubes.

2. Place the natto, naganegi, ground pork and combined (A) in a bowl (photo 1), and mix well until the meat becomes sticky.

3. Spread the shaomai wrapper on a ring made with thumb and forefinger and stuff **2** into it (photo 2), adjusting the shape. Top each with corn, green peas, shiitake and shrimp respectively.

4. Place a cooking sheet in a steaming steamer. Arrange **3** (photo 3) and steam over high heat 10 minutes.

Stir-fried Toasted Tofu

Ingredients (4 servings)

2 blocks toasted tofu
4 stalks chingensai (bok choy)
1 tsp salt
1 Tbsp cornstarch

4 Tbsp oil
(A)
- ⅓ cup oyster sauce
- 2 Tbsp sake
- 1 tsp sugar
- pinch sesame oil

[Calories 278 kcal., Protein 13.3 g]

Method: 1. Cut a block of tofu in half lengthwise and then into ½″ (1.5 cm) thickness. Cut the chingensai in half.

2. Heat 2 Tbsp oil in a pan and fry the chingensai. Add salt and 2 cups boiled water and cover with a lid. When it becomes tender, take out and drain.

3. Heat 2 Tbsp oil in a pan and brown both sides of tofu and remove. Combine (A) in a pan and bring to a boil. Return the tofu to the pan. Add the cornstarch dissolved in 2 Tbsp water and thicken. Serve on a plate garnished with the chingensai.

Noodles Topped with Natto & Nira

Ingredients (4 servings)

2 packs natto (femented
  soybeans)
1 bunch nira (a type of leek)
½ naganegi (Japanese leek)
5 eggs
4 balls steamed Chinese
  noodles

3 Tbsp sesame oil
(A) {
  some Chinese soup
    base (granules)
  1⅓ Tbsp shoyu
  1⅓ Tbsp salt
  1⅓ Tbsp sesame oil
}

[Calories 627 kcal., Protein 23.7 g]

Method: 1. Cut the nira into ¾″ (2 cm) lengths. Mince the naganegi coarsely.

2. Add the natto to beaten eggs and mix with chopsticks (photo). Add the nira and naganegi.

3. Heat oil in a frying pan. Pour in **2**, stirring with chopsticks, and cook soft scrambled eggs.

4. Place 8 cups water and combined (A) in a saucepan and bring to a boil. Add the noodles. Serve in a bowl topped with scrambled eggs.

Green Soup of Tofu

Ingredients (4 servings)

1 block kinugoshi-dofu
  (silken tofu)
1 bunch spinach
1 clove garlic
1 piece ginger
1 Tbsp cornstarch

(A) {
  some Chinese soup
    base (granules)
  2 Tbsp sake
  1 tsp shoyu
}
2 Tbsp sesame oil

[Calories 171 kcal., Protein 6.5 g]

Method: 1. Cut the tofu into bite-sized pieces. Parboil the spinach, transfer to cold water, drain and mince. Mince the garlic and ginger.

2. Heat the sesame oil in a saucepan and stir-fry the garlic and ginger. Add 4 cups water and combined (A) (photo). Add the spinach and bring to a boil. Add the cornstarch dissolved in 2 Tbsp water.

3. Using another saucepan, heat the tofu in boiling water. Drain and place in a bowl. Pour in **2**.

Fried Rice with Tofu

Ingredients (4 servings)

1 block momen-dofu (firm tofu)	$\frac{3}{4}$ oz (20 g) small shrimp
4$\frac{1}{4}$ oz (120 g) roast pork	4 bowls of cooked rice
$\frac{1}{2}$ naganegi (Japanese leek)	2～3 chives
	1 tsp salt
1 Tbsp pine nuts	1 tsp shoyu
	3 Tbsp sesame oil

[Calories 486 kcal., Protein 19.2 g]

Method: 1. Drain the tofu as directed on page 4. Wrap in a dish towel and squeeze out water. Cut the roast pork into $\frac{1}{4}''$ (7 mm) cubes. Cut the naganegi and chives into thin round slices.

2. Heat the oil in a pan and stir-fry the naganegi and shrimp. Add the tofu(photo). When the tofu crumbles, add the pork, cooked rice and pine nuts in this order, stir-frying.

3. Season with salt and shoyu. Place on a plate and sprinkle with chives.

Chinese-style Salad with Koori-dofu

Ingredients (4 servings)

3 pieces koori-dofu (freeze-dried tofu)	Dressing
1 cucumber	3 Tbsp dashi stock
$\frac{1}{2}$ carrot	4″ (10 cm) naganegi (Japanese leek)
5～6 mitsuba (honewort)	1 small clove garlic
$\frac{1}{2}$ lettuce	$\frac{1}{3}$ piece ginger
	3 Tbsp shoyu
	2 Tbsp vinegar
	1 Tbsp sugar
	2 Tbsp sesame oil

[Calories 156 kcal., Protein 7.7 g]

Method: 1. Reconstitute the koori-dofu as directed on page 5. Drain and cut into thin rectangles. Peel the cucumber and carrot, and cut into julienne strips. Cut the mitsuba into 1$\frac{1}{2}''$ (4 cm) lengths. Tear the lettuce into bite-sized pieces.

2. Make the dressing. Mince the naganegi garlic and ginger, and combine with the other ingredients (photo).

3. Arrange **1** on a plate colorfully and pour the dressing over.

Okara & Prune Cookie

Ingredients (25 pieces)

$3\frac{1}{2}$ oz (100 g) okara (tofu lees)
$5\frac{1}{4}$ oz (150 g) pastry flour
$2\frac{3}{4}$ oz (80 g) butter
$2\frac{3}{4}$ oz (80 g) sugar
1 egg
$3\frac{1}{2}$ oz (100 g) dried prune
1 Tbsp brandy

[Calories 1,908 kcal., Protein 26.5 g] in all

Method: 1. Sift the flour. Soften the butter at room temperature.

2. Toast the okara as directed on page 5. Cut the prunes into fine pieces and sprinkle with brandy.

3. Cream the butter in a bowl. Add the sugar and mix well until it turns whitish. Add the beaten egg gradually and mix (photo 1). Add the okara and flour and mix well.

4. Add the prune to the half amount of **3** (photo 2) and knead the mixture until it becomes evenly brown.

5. On plastic wrap, spread the remaining half of **3** in a rectangle, $\frac{3}{8}''$ (1 cm) thick. Place **4** shaped elliptically in the center (photo 3). Roll up together with the wrap and store in the refrigerator for $1\sim2$ hours.

6. Cut **5** into pieces, $\frac{1}{8}''$ (4 mm) thick. Arrange on a wax paper placed on a tray. Bake at 360°F (180°C) in an oven for $18\sim20$ minutes.

Sponge Cake of Koori-dofu

Ingredients (8″×2¾″×2¼″/20×7×6 cm)

3 pieces koori-dofu
  (freeze-dried tofu)
(A) { ¾ oz (20 g) almond
      powder
      1 tsp baking powder
3 eggs

⅓ cup sugar
2 Tbsp melted butter
almond slices, butter,
pastry flour, mint

[Calories 1,011 kcal., Protein 51.3 g] in all

Method: 1. Grind the koori-dofu in a food processor (photo 1) and sieve together with (A).
2. Beat eggs with a hand mixer until white-colored and foamy and add the sugar (photo 2). Add **1** all at one time and mix well with a wooden spatula. Lastly, add melted butter (photo 3) and stir to mix.
3. Butter a mold and lightly flour. Pour in **2** (photo 4). Top with sliced almonds and bake at 360°F (180°C) in an oven for 20~30 minutes.

Tofu & Powdered Green Tea Dumpling

Ingredients (4 servings)

½ block kinugoshi-dofu
4¼ oz (120 g) shiratamako

2~3 tsp matcha
7 oz (200 g) boiled adzuki beans

[Calories 234 kcal., Protein 6.6 g]

Method: 1. Rince the tofu in water quickly and cut into 3 or 4 portions.
2. Combine the tofu, shiratamako, and matcha in a bowl (photo). Knead with force until the dough becomes the consistency of your earlobes.
3. Break **2** up into small dumplings. Indent the center with a finger place in boiling water.
4. When the dumplings come up to the surface, continue boiling another 1~2 minutes and then transfer to cold water. Drain and serve on a plate with adzuki.

Tofu Dishes from OKINAWA

Okinawa is said to have the largest number of long-lived people in Japan. A great many spry old people enjoy longevity there. Okinawa abounds in a variety of tofu dishes. Local specialties make use of pork and bitter melon.

Goya Champuru

Ukarairichi

Ujira-tofu

Goya Champuru

Ingredients (4 servings)

2 blocks momen-dofu (firm tofu)	1 Tbsp sake
½ nigauri (bitter melon)	1 tsp shoyu
¼ oz (6 g) dried bonito flakes	2 Tbsp sesame oil
	salt, pepper, toasted sesame seeds (white)

[Calories 209 kcal., Protein 12.3 g]

Method: 1. Drain the tofu as directed on page 4. Cut the nigauri in half lengthwise and take out the seeds and insides with a spoon. Cut into thin slices (photo). Sprinkle with salt and make pliable. Squeeze out the juice. **2.** Heat 1 Tbsp sesame oil in a pan and stir-fry the tofu over a brisk flame. Season with a pinch of salt and pepper. Remove from the pan.

3. Heat 1 Tbsp sesame oil in a pan and stir-fry the nigauri. Add the tofu and bonito flakes and stir to mix. Season with a pinch of sake, shoyu, salt and pepper. Place on a plate and sprinkle with sesame seeds to serve.

Ukarairichi

Ingredients (4 servings)

7 oz (200 g) okara (tofu lees)	1¾ oz (50 g) kamaboko (boiled fish paste)
3 dried shiitake mushrooms	½ bunch scallions
⅛ oz (3 g) cloud ear mushrooms	3 Tbsp sugar
3½ oz (100 g) thin slices of pork	3 Tbsp shoyu
	1 Tbsp vinegar
	3 Tbsp oil

[Calories 239 kcal., Protein 9.8 g]

Method: 1. Cover the shiitake and cloud ear with water and reconstitute. Drain. Cut off the stems of shiitake. Cut the shiitake and cloud ear into julienne strips. Reserve the water in which the shiitake was soaked.

2. Cut the pork into ⅜" (1 cm) wide pieces. Cut the kamaboko into thin rectangles. Cut scallions into 1¼" (3 cm) lengths. **3.** Heat the oil in a pan and stir-fry the pork. When the color changes, add the shiitake and cloud ear and continue stir-frying. Add the okara, and stir-fry until it comes to pieces. Pour in 1 cup of water plus the shiitake-soaking water. **4.** Add the sugar, shoyu and vinegar and stir to mix occasionally. Simmer over moderate heat until half of the liquid has gone. **5.** Add the kamaboko and scallions and simmer until all the liquid has been evaporated. Serve on a plate.

Ujira-tofu

Ingredients (4 servings)

2 blocks momen-dofu (firm tofu)	salt, oil for deep-fry
⅛ oz (3 g) cloud ear mushrooms	(A) { 1¾ oz (50 g) canned tuna
⅓ carrot	½ Tbsp peanut butter (sugarless)
¾ oz (20 g) snow peas	1 egg
some dashi stock	1 Tbsp ground sesame seeds (black)
½ tsp shoyu	1 tsp salt

[Calories 328 kcal., Protein 17.2 g]

Method: 1. Cover the cloud ear with water, reconstitute and drain. Cut the cloud ear and carrot into fine strips. **2.** Drain the tofu as directed on page 4. String snow peas and boil in salted water. Drain and cut into julienne strips. **3.** Place the dashi stock and shoyu in a saucepan and bring to a boil. Add the cloud ear and carrot and simmer about 10 minutes.

4. Combine the tofu and (A) in a food processor (photo) and stir to mix until smooth. Transfer to a bowl. Add snow peas, drained cloud ear and carrot and mix well. **5.** Scoop with a wooden ladle and adjust the shape. Preheat the oil to 340°F (170°C) and deep-fry until browned.

★This is an Okinawa-style 'ganmodoki' (deep-fried tofu with vegetables). The peanut butter enhances the savory taste.

Chapter 3

OTHER FOODS PROCESSED FROM SOYBEANS

Here are foods processed from soybeans in addition to tofu, natto and okara, atsu-age, miso, yuba, soymilk, soybean flour — they vary in appearance, but all are made from soybeans. Enjoy the many tastes of soybeans.

Atsu-age

Momen-dofu (firm tofu); well drained and deep-fried over a high heat. Whatever methods are employed, grilled or boiled, the shape remains, so it can be used in many ways. Atsu-age contains about twice as much protein as tofu.

Gadogado Salad

Ingredients (4 servings)

2 blocks atsu-age
  (thick deep-fried tofu)
½ bunch spinach
  (for salad)
4 cabbage leaves
1 tomato
2 eggs
⅓ small onion
1 clove small garlic
1 red chili pepper
1 Tbsp cumin seeds

(A)
- 1 Tbsp oyster sauce
- 1 Tbsp tomato ketchup
- 1 Tbsp shoyu
- 6 Tbsp peanut butter (sugarless)
- 3 Tbsp lemon juice
- 1 tsp ginger juice
- 1 tsp sugar
- ½ tsp salt
- pinch pepper
- 2 Tbsp oil

[Calories 509 kcal., Protein 26.8 g]

Method: 1. Remove oil from the atsu-age in the same way as done for abura-age on page 5. Drain and cut into ¾″ (2 cm) cubes.
2. Cut off the roots of the spinach. Cut the cabbage into thick strips. Cut the tomato in wedges. Hard boil eggs, shell and cut into quarters.
3. Grate the onion and garlic. Soak the chili pepper in water and soften. Drain and seed. Toast the cumin lightly to taste.
4. Grind the chili pepper and cumin in an earthenware mortar. Combine the onion, garlic and (A) and mix, grinding.
5. Arrange the atsu-age and **2** on a plate. Pour sauce **4** over to serve.

Gadogado Salad

Cheese Piccata

Cheese Piccata

Ingredients (4 servings)

2 blocks atsu-age (thick deep-fried tofu)	pinch salt
3 Tbsp pastry flour	2 Tbsp butter
3 eggs	1 Tbsp oil
2 Tbsp minced parsley	pepper, cherry tomato, watercress
3 Tbsp powdered cheese	

[Calories 361 kcal., Protein 20.0 g]

Method: 1. Remove oil from the atsu-age in the same way as done for abura-age on page 5. Drain and cut into pieces, ⅜″ (1 cm) thick.

2. Break eggs into a bowl. Add the minced parsley, powdered cheese, a pinch of pepper and beat.

3. Sprinkle the atsu-age with a pinch of salt and pepper and dust with the flour. Heat the butter and oil in a frying pan. Dip the atsu-age in **2** (photo) and fry over medium heat.

4. When the whole is browned, place on a plate and serve with cherry tomatoes and watercress.

Fried Atsu-age with Sweet Vinegar

Ingredients (4 servings)

2 blocks atsu-age
  (thick deep-fried tofu)
$3\frac{1}{2}$ oz (100 g) slices of pork
1 pack shimeji mushrooms
1 naganegi (Japanese leek)
$\frac{1}{2}$ carrot
2 green peppers
1 clove garlic
1 piece small ginger

$1\frac{1}{2}$ Tbsp cornstarch
2 Tbsp oil

(A) {
1 cup soup
3 Tbsp sugar
2 Tbsp shoyu
2 Tbsp vinegar
1 Tbsp oyster sauce
1 Tbsp lemon juice
pinch salt, pepper
}

[Calories 346 kcal., Protein 18.3 g]

Method: 1. Remove oil from the atsu-age in the same way as done for abura-age on page 5. Drain and cut in half lengthwise and then diagonally into bite-sized pieces. **2.** Cut the pork into pieces, $1\frac{1}{4}''$ (3 cm) wide. Cut away root clusters of the shimeji and separate them. Cut the naganegi diagonally. Cut the carrot into thin rectangles, $1\frac{1}{4}''$ (3 cm) long. Cut the green pepper into bite-sized pieces. Crush the garlic and mince the ginger. **3.** Heat the oil in a pan and stir-fry the garlic and ginger until aromatic. Add the pork. When the pork changes the color, add the remaining vegetables and atsu-age (photo 1) and continue stir-frying. **4.** Add combined (A) and bring to a boil (photo 2). Thicken with the cornstarch dissolved in 3 Tbsp water.

Atsu-age, Greens & Young Sardines

Ingredients (4 servings)

1 block atsu-age (thick
  deep-fried tofu)
1 bunch komatsuna (brassica rapa)
2 Tbsp chirimenjako
  (dried young sardines)

1 tsp oil
Sauce
{
$1\frac{1}{2}$ cup dashi stock
2 Tbsp sake
2 Tbsp shoyu
2 Tbsp mirin
}

[Calories 159 kcal., Protein 12.0 g]

Method: 1. Remove oil from the atsu-age in the same way as done for abura-age on page 5. Drain and cut in half lengthwise and then into 8 portions. Parboil the komatsuna and transfer to cold water. Drain and cut into $1\frac{1}{2}''$ (4 cm) lengths.

2. Heat the oil in a frying pan and stir-fry the chirimenjako until crisp.

3. Place the sauce and atsu-age in a saucepan and simmer over medium heat 5~6 minutes. Add the komatsuna and bring to a boil.

4. Place the atsu-age and komatsuna in a bowl and top with the chirimenjako.

★This dish provides more than half of the amount of calcium necessary for a day.

Develop Tireless Strength

If you take three meals a day just for satisfying your appetite, it does not follow that you get enough nutrition from your diet. If you feel tired or depressed, the cause often lies in an unbalanced diet. You should reflect on your daily dietary habits.

If you want to relieve your fatigue or to increase your vitality, you should take high quality protein. Soybeans and foods processed from them contain protein of good quality, and fermented foods like natto and miso and soybeans flour are especially easily and effectively assimilated into the body.

It is often said that liver is good for anemia. This is because liver contains iron, protein and such minerals as copper and magnesium. Similarly, soybeans have a variety of nutrients. They don't have a distinct taste like liver, and foods processed from them like miso and natto are palatable to the taste of our everyday meals.

As a tidbit taken with alcoholic drinks, soybeans are ideal for those who drink alcohol often or those who are suffering from liver trouble. The food that improves the function of liver contains high-protein and low fat, so it is the basics of a healthy diet. You should avoid such high-fat foods as processed meat like ham and salami and nuts. Low-fat foods ease the liver.

The lecithin in soybeans is effective in preventing a fatty liver. The mucin in natto protects the walls of the stomach from the irritation of alcohol and vitamin B_2 improves the function of liver.

Chinese Cheese "FURU"

'Furu' is a fermented tofu made with condiments and spices added. It is a unique Chinese food which has a characteristic rich taste and it is called 'cheese in China.' Generally, it is eaten with rice gruel or with alcoholic drinks or used in place of pickles. There are several kinds of 'furu' according to the condiments and spices added, and they are divided into two groups, white and red.

HON-FURU (above): Fermented with wine added. It has a refreshing taste.
RA-FURU (center): Fermented with chili pepper added. The pungent taste goes well with rice gruel.
MYAJAN-FURU (below): Fermented with rice added. It has a strong salty taste.

ABURA-AGE

Abura-age is a thin slice of tofu deep-fried in oil at a low temperature. Since the inside is hollow, it is possible to cut sides to make pouches and fill with other ingredients or open it flat and roll the ingredients up. It is applicable in various shapes. You should choose the one, which is evenly thick and not too firm.

Abura-age & Julienne Vegetables

Ingredients (4 servings)

4 abura-age
½ daikon radish
1 small carrot
1 bunch scallions
7 oz (200 g) fresh shiitake
  mushrooms
1 pack enoki mushrooms

[Calories 184 kcal., Protein 9.1 g]

Sauce

6 cups dashi stock
2 Tbsp sake
1 Tbsp shoyu
1 Tbsp mirin
1 tsp salt

shichimi-tougarashi
  (seven-spice pepper)

Method: 1. Remove oil from the abura-age as directed on page 5. Drain and cut into strips, ¼" (5 mm) wide.

2. Cut the daikon and carrot into julienne strips, 2" (5 cm) long. Cut the scallions into 2¾" (7 cm) lengths. Remove the stems of shiitake and cut into thin slices. Cut away the root clusters of enoki mushrooms and separate them.

3. Bring the sauce to a boil in an earthenware pot. Add the abura-age and vegetables. When it comes to a boil, transfer to a bowl and sprinkle with shichimi to serve.

★You may cook quickly so that the vegetables remain firm, or simmer until they become soft. Either method tastes nice.

Zenmai Rolled in Abura-age

Ingredients (4 servings)

4 abura-age
7 oz (200 g) zenmai (flowering fern) (boiled plain)
½ oz (15 g) kampyo (dried gourd strips)
½ bunch spinach
2¾ oz (80 g) namafu (wheat gluten)
Sauce
{ 2 cups dashi stock
{ 2 Tbsp shoyu
{ 2 Tbsp mirin
pinch cornstarch
[Calories 216 kcal., Protein 10.8 g]

Method: 1. Remove oil from abura-age and drain. Cut three edges and open. **2.** Rinse kampyo in water and parboil. Drain. Parboil spinach, transfer to cold water, squeeze out water and cut into 1¼″ (3 cm) lengths. **3.** Spread the abura-age inside out and sprinkle with cornstarch. Place zenmai in the center (photo 1). Roll all the way up and tie at three points loosely with the kampyo (photo 2). Make other 3 rolls same way. **4.** Place the sauce and **3** in a pot and bring to a boil over medium heat. Lower the heat, place a small lid on the food (photo 3) and simmer about 15 minutes. **5.** Cut the roll into 3 portions with the kampyo tie in the center and place on a plate. Cook the spinach and namafu in the remaining sauce quickly and serve with the sauce.

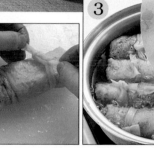

Grilled Abura-age

Ingredients (4 servings)

4 abura-age
½ naganegi (Japanese leek)
⅜ oz (10 g) dried bonito flakes
3½ oz (100 g) daikon radish
1 red chili pepper
lemon, shoyu

[Calories 134 kcal., Protein 8.1 g]

Method: 1. Remove oil from the abura-age as directed on page 5 and drain. Cut in half sideways and carefully open to make pouches.
2. Cut the naganegi into fine pieces and mix with bonito flakes.
3. Soak the chili pepper in water until tender and seed. Pare the daikon and make a hole in the center with a chopstick and insert the chili pepper in it. Grate and lightly drain.
4. Stuff **2** into the pouches equally and place on a heated grill. Grill both sides until the surface gets slightly burned. Place on a plate with **3** and the lemon slice cut into a wedge. Dip in shoyu before eating.

MISO

Miso is made from a combination of steamed soybeans and a grain such as rice or barley. It is fermented with a special bacteria(koji). The distinct and complex flavor varies according to the regions and climate where it is produced. Especially those made from soybeans contain plenty of protein and calcium and have a delicate taste.

Chilled Cucumber Soup

Ingredients (4 servings)

1 cucumber
1 horse mackerel
10 aojiso (green shiso leaves)
1¾ oz (50 g) kaiware
  (daikon sprouts)
2 Tbsp toasted sesame
  seeds (white)
3 Tbsp miso (salty)
3 cups dashi stock
salt, ice

[Calories 88 kcal., Protein 6.8 g]

Method: 1. Allow the dashi stock to chill.
2. Peel the cucumber in places and cut into thin slices. Cut the aojiso in half lengthwise and then into julienne strips. Cut away the roots of kaiware and cut in half.
3. Remove entrails of the horse mackerel (photo 1). Rinse well in running water. Pat dry and sprinkle with a pinch of salt. Grill on a heated grill until light brown. Remove the skin, bones and then break up into pieces.

4. Grind the sesame seeds until sticky. Add the fish and miso mix, grinding (photo 2). Gradually add the dashi stock, stirring (photo 3) until smooth.
5. Add cucumber slices, a pinch of salt and season to taste.
6. Place in a bowl and scatter the aojiso and kaiware over. Add ice, stir lightly, and serve chilled.

Dried Daikon with Miso Mayonnaise

Braised Chicken & Daikon

Braised Chicken & Daikon

Ingredients (4 servings)

1 chicken thigh
Seasoning
{ 1 tsp shoyu
{ 1 tsp sake
4 dried shiitake mush-
    rooms
14 oz (400 g) daikon radish
½ carrot

2 oz (60 g) string beans
1 cup dashi stock
(A) { 2 oz (60 g) miso (mild)
     { 1 Tbsp sugar
     { 1 Tbsp sake
     { 1 Tbsp toasted
         sesame seeds (white)
1 Tbsp shoyu
1 Tbsp oil

[Calories 220 kcal., Protein 15.3 g]

Method: 1. Cut the chicken into bite-sized pieces and season with shoyu and sake. Cover the shiitake with water and reconstitute. Cut away the stems and cut into bite-sized pieces. Reserve the shiitake soaked water. Cut the daikon and carrot diagonally, rotating. Parboil the string beans quickly, drain and cut in half. **2.** Heat the oil in a pan and stir-fry the chicken over medium heat. When the color turns brown, add all the vegetable except string beans, and continue stir-frying. Add the dashi stock and the shiitake-soaking water and bring to a boil. Combine (A), add and simmer over low heat about 20 minutes with a small lid resting directly on the food.
3. Add the string beans and shoyu and raise the flame, covering the whole with the shoyu.

Dried Daikon with Miso Mayonnaise

Ingredients (4 servings)

1½ oz (40 g) dried strips
   of daikon radish
1 sheet kombu kelp
   (4″ (10 cm) square)
½ carrot

1 cucumber
Miso mayonnaise
{ 1½ Tbsp miso
{ 4 Tbsp mayonnaise
leaf lettuce, salt

[Calories 149 kcal., Protein 3.0 g]

Method: 1. Rinse the dried strips of daikon radish in water. Cover the kombu kelp and daikon with water and allow to stand for 15~20 minutes to reconstitute. Parboil in hot water quickly. Squeeze out water and cut into bite-sized pieces.
2. Cut the carrot and cucumber into julienne strips, ¾″ (2 cm) long. Sprinkle with salt and let stand until pliable. Squeeze out juice completely.
3. Mix the miso and mayonnaise and dress the daikon, carrot and cucumber (photo).
4. Tear the leaf lettuce into bite-sized pieces and spread on a plate. Place **3** to serve.

SOY MILK

Soy milk contains almost all the nutrients soybeans have. It is a source of protein that is easy to digest and be absorbed. It has recently been discovered that the protein of soybeans is almost perfect for adults. Let's try to take in the degestible soy milk to prevent adult diseases.

Littleneck Clam Chowder

Ingredients (4 servings)

14 oz (400 g) littleneck clams
½ large onion
½ carrot
2 potatoes
1 cup corns (canned)

2 Tbsp pastry flour
1 bouillon cube
2 cups soy milk
pinch pepper
2 Tbsp butter
salt, minced parsley

[Calories 224 kcal., Protein 10.1 g]

Method: 1. Let the clams stand in slightly salted water to allow them to expel sand. Transfer to a bamboo colander and drain.
2. Cut the onion into ¼″ (8 mm) cubes, the carrot into ⅜″ (1 cm) cubes and the potatoes into ¾″ (2 cm) cubes. Drain the corn.

3. Heat the butter in a pot and stir-fry the onion over medium heat until transparent. Add the flour and stir-fry carefully not to burn. Add 2 cups water and the bouillon cube and bring to a boil.
4. Add the carrot and potatoes and cook until tender. Add the littleneck clams and corn and cook 3~4 minutes, skimming the surface to remove foam. Add the soy milk (photo). Season with ½ tsp salt and pepper.
5. Place in a bowl and sprinkle with minced parsley.

Carrot Potage

Ingredients (4 servings)

2 carrots	½ Tbsp sugar
1 small onion	pinch pepper
2 bouillon cubes	3 Tbsp butter
2 Tbsp rice	salt, oil for frying
2 cups soy milk	minced parsley
½ slice of bread	
(cut into 8 slices)	

[Calories 236 kcal., Protein 5.8 g]

Method: 1. Cut the carrot and onion into thin slices.
2. Melt the butter in a thick pot and stir-fry **1** over medium heat with care not to burn (photo 1). Stir in 2 Tbsp water, sugar and 1 tsp salt. Lower the heat and cover with a lid. Simmer about 5 minutes.
3. Add 4 cups water, bouillon cubes and rice (photo 2) and cook over moderate heat. When the rice is cooked tender, remove from the heat. When it is cooled, blend in a blender (photo 3).
4. Return **3** to a pot and add the soy milk and bring to a boil. Season with a pinch of salt and pepper.
5. Cut the bread into ¼″ (8 mm) cubes, and deep-fry in the oil at 320°F (160°C).
6. Place **4** in a bowl and sprinkle with **5** and minced parsely.

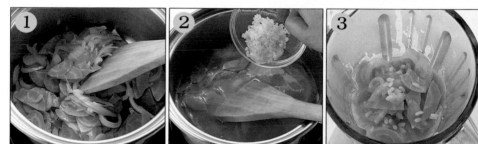

Chinese-style Soy Milk Soup

Ingredients (4 servings)

1 tomato	1 cup soy milk
3 eggs	1 Tbsp sesame oil
1 tsp Chinese soup base	2~3 scallions
(granules)	

[Calories 131 kcal., Protein 7.4 g]

Method: 1. Make a criss-cross cut on the skin of the tomato. Soak in boiling water and then peel. Cut into bite-sized pieces. Chop the scallions.
2. Heat the sesame oil in a frying pan. Beat in eggs, stirring with a chopstick, and cook into soft scrambled eggs.
3. Place 2 cups water, soy milk and soup base in a pot and bring to a boil. Add the tomato. When the tomato is cooked, stir in the scrambled eggs.
4. Place in a bowl and sprinkle with the scallions.

YUBA
(Dried Soybeans Casein)

Yuba is made from layer upon layer of the skin which forms on top of thick soy milk as it is simmered. What is scooped up and drained is fresh yuba and what is air dried is dried yuba. Either yuba has a plain and characteristic taste. Dried yuba is broken up and used in batter for deep-frying.

Yuba with Vinegared Sesame

Ingredients (4 servings)

¾ oz (20 g) dried yuba
1 pack shimeji mush-rooms
3½ oz (100 g) mitsuba (honewort)
4 imitation crab made of boiled fish paste

Sauce
⎰ ½ cup dashi stock
⎱ 1 Tbsp sake
⎱ ½ Tbsp shoyu
Vinegared sesame
⎰ 2 Tbsp toasted sesame seeds (white)
⎱ 2 Tbsp vinegar
⎱ 1 Tbsp sugar
⎱ 1 tsp shoyu
⎱ ⅓ tsp salt

[Calories 114 kcal., Protein 8.1 g]

Method: 1. Place the yuba in a bamboo colander. Pour lukewarm water over and reconstitute. Drain and cut into bite-sized pieces. **2.** Cut away root clusters of the shimeji and separate them. Pour hot water over the mitsuba briefly. Drain and cut into 1¼" (3 cm) lengths. Tear the imitation crab into fine sticks. **3.** Bring the sauce to a boil in a pot. Add the shimeji and simmer over low heat for 5~6 minutes until well seasoned. **4.** Combine the vinegared sesame ingredients and dress the yuba, drained shimeji, mitsuba and imitation crab.

★You may use 2 oz (60 g) of fresh yuba in place of dried yuba.

Yuba with Cod Roe & Milk

Ingredients (4 servings)

3½ oz (100 g) fresh yuba
1 cod roe
5 scallions
½ piece ginger
1 red chili pepper

(A) ⎰ 2½ cups milk
⎱ 1 tsp dashi base (granule)
1½ Tbsp cornstarch
pinch salt
1 tsp oil
sake

[Calories 177 kcal., Protein 13.1 g]

Method: 1. Cut the yuba into ¾" (2 cm) cubes. Cut the cod roe in half sideways and then make an incision lengthwise and draw the inside out. Season with 1 Tbsp sake.
2. Chop the scallions and mince the ginger. Soak the chili pepper in water and soften. Seed and chop.
3. Heat the oil in a pot and stir-fry **2**. Add (A) and 1 Tbsp sake and mix. Add the yuba and cod roe and bring to a boil. Simmer over low heat for 2~3 minutes and add salt. Add the cornstarch dissolved in 3 Tbsp water and thicken.

Deep-fried Yuba & Chicken Breasts

Ingredients (4 servings)

7 oz (200 g) chicken breasts
Seasoning
⎰ ½ tsp salt
⎱ 1 Tbsp sake
12 small green peppers

some pastry flour
1 small egg
1½" oz (40 g) dried yuba
salt, oil for deep-frying, lemon

[Calories 196 kcal., Protein 18.8 g]

Method: 1. Remove stringy membrane from the chicken breasts, cut diagonally into bite-sized pieces and season with salt and sake. Make incisions in the green peppers. **2.** Place the yuba in a plastic bag and crush with hands (photo 1). **3.** Drain the chicken breasts briefly. Dust lightly with flour, dip in beaten egg and dredge with the crushed yuba (photo 2). **4.** Preheat oil to 340°F (170°C). Deep-fry **3** until golden (photo 3). Lower the temperature to 320°F (160°C), deep-fry green peppers crisp and sprinkle with salt. **5.** Serve the chicken breasts and green peppers on a plate garnished with lemon wedges.

Yuba with
Vinegared Sesame

Yuba with
Cod Roe & Milk

Deep-fried Yuba &
Chicken Breasts

DAIZU MOYASHI
(Soybeans Sprouts)

Moyashi are bean sprouts. Soybean sprouts are a rich source of minerals and vitamins, especially vitamin C which soybeans do not have. If cooked for a short time, they remain crunchy and have special flavored taste while retaining vitamins.

Moyashi Salad

Ingredients (4 servings)

2 packs soybeans sprouts
Thin Omelet
⎧ 2 eggs
⎨ pinch sugar, salt
⎩ dash cornstarch, oil
1 cucumber
4 slices ham made of pork loin
¼ carrot
½ red onion
Dipping Sauce
⎧ 2 Tbsp dashi stock
⎪ 1 Tbsp toasted sesame
⎪   seeds (white)
⎨ 1 Tbsp vinegar
⎪ 1 tsp sugar
⎪ 1 Tbsp shoyu
⎩ 1 Tbsp sesame oil

[Calories 182 kcal., Protein 12.9 g]

Method: 1. Remove root hairs of the soybean sprouts. Parboil in hot water. Transfer to a bamboo colander and drain.
2. Beat the eggs. Mix in the sugar, salt and cornstarch. Heat the oil in a frying pan. Pour in the egg mixture and cook a thin omelet. Spread on a bamboo colander and allow to cool. Cut the omelet in fine strips.
3. Cut the ham, carrot and onion into julienne strips. Cut the red onion into slices and soak in water for a while and drain.
4. Combine the ingredients of the dipping sauce and mix well.
5. Arrange on a plate and pour the sauce over.

Moyashi & Mentaiko

Ingredient (4 servings)

lettuce

1 pack soybean sprouts
3~4 scallions
10 aojiso (green shiso leaves)
1 mentaiko (salted ovary of pollack)

(A)
- 1 Tbsp vinegar
- 1 Tbsp shoyu
- ½ tsp sugar
- ½ tsp salt
- pinch pepper
- 1 Tbsp sesame oil

[Calories 99 kcal., Protein 8.6 g]

Method: 1. Remove root hairs of the soybean sprouts (photo 1). Parboil in hot water briefly. Transfer to a bamboo colander and drain.
2. Chop scallions and cut aojiso into julienne.
3. Cut the mentaiko in half sideways and then make an incision lengthwise and draw the inside out (photo 2). Reserve a pinch of it for topping.
4. Combine (A) and mix well (photo 3). Stir in the mentaiko. Dress the soybean sprouts with the mixture. Place on the lettuce arranged in a bowl. Scatter the scallions and aojiso over and top with the reserved mentaiko.

Curry & Moyashi

Ingredients (4 servings)

1 pack soybean sprouts
1 cucumber
1 oz (30 g) raisins

(A)
- 2 tsp curry powder
- 1 Tbsp sesame oil
- ½ tsp salt
- pinch sugar

[Calories 115 kcal., Protein 4.6 g]

Method: 1. Remove root hairs of the soybean sprouts. Parboil in hot water so that they remain firm. Transfer to a bamboo colander and drain.
2. Cut the cucumber in julienne strips. Wash the raisins briefly and drain.
3. Combine (A) and mix well. Dress the soybean sprouts, cucumber and raisins with the mixture.

★The sweetness of raisins goes well with the taste of curry. It is also nice to substitute minced dried prunes for the raisins.

KINAKO
(Soybean Flour)

Toasted soybeans are ground into flour. There are two varieties of flour, the one made from yellow soybeans and the other from green soybeans. Since water is not used, there is no fear of nutrients running out, and it may help prevent hypertension and colon cancer.

Potato Rice Cake coated with Kinako

Ingredients (4 servings)

1 large sweet potato 2 Tbsp sugar
1 piece mochi (glutinous rice cake) green soybean flour
[Calories 130 kcal., Protein 2.9 g]

Method: 1. Cut the sweet potato into ring slices. Peel the skin thickly and soak in water to remove the acrid taste. Drain.
2. Place in a preheated steamer and steam over high heat for about 10 minutes.
3. Insert a skewer into the sweet potato and if it comes out clean, add the mochi and steam for another 2~3 minutes until tender.
4. Place the sweet potato and mochi in an earthenware mortar, and mash, stirring. Add 1 ~2 Tbsp soybean flour and sugar.
5. Knead until the dough becomes as soft as your earlobes. Divide into 8 portions. Form into an oval shape and coat the whole with the soybean flour.

* * *

Twisted Kinako

Ingredients (4 servings)

3½ Tbsp rice syrup soybean flour
[Calories 140 kcal., Protein 6.2 g]

Method: 1. Place the rice syrup in a heatproof dish and soften by heating in a microwave oven for 1 minute.
2. Add 1¾ oz (50 g) soybean flour and blend well until smooth with a wooden spatula.
3. Sprinkle a board sparsely with the soybean flour and place **2** on it. Roll out the mixture to a ¼″ (5 mm) thickness (photo). Cut into square pieces, ¾″ (2 cm) × 1½″ (4 cm). Twist like a ribbon and coat with the soybean flour.

★If you keep it in a airtight container, and put it in a cool place, it can be kept as long as 3~4 days.